LIAM O'FLAHERTY

A Study of the Short Fiction

Also available in Twayne's Studies in Short Fiction Series

Twayne's Studies in Short Fiction

Gordon Weaver, General Editor
Oklahoma State University

Liam O'Flaherty in 1952 at age fifty-six. *Reprinted with the permission of Lensmen Limited, Dublin.*

LIAM O'FLAHERTY

————— *A Study of the Short Fiction* —————

James M. Cahalan
Indiana University of Pennsylvania

TWAYNE PUBLISHERS • BOSTON
A Division of G. K. Hall & Co.

Twayne's Studies in Short Fiction Series No. 23

Copyright 1991 by G. K. Hall & Co.
All rights reserved.
Published by Twayne Publishers
A division of G. K. Hall & Co.
70 Lincoln Street
Boston, Massachusetts 02111

Copyediting supervised by Barbara Sutton.
Book design and production by Janet Z. Reynolds.
Typeset in Caslon 540 by Compset, Inc., Beverly, Massachusetts.

First published 1991.
10 9 8 7 6 5 4 3 2 1

The paper used in this publication meets the minimum requirements
of American National Standard for Information Sciences—Permanence
of Paper for Printed Library Materials, ANSI Z39.48-1984. ∞"

Printed and bound in the United States of America.

Library of Congress Cataloging-in-Publication Data
Cahalan, James M.
      Liam O'Flaherty : a study of the short fiction / James M. Cahalan.
      p.   —(Twayne's studies in short fiction ; no. 23)
      Includes bibliographical references and index.
      ISBN 0-8057-8312-1
      1. O'Flaherty, Liam, 1896-   —Criticism and interpretation.
      2. Ireland in literature.   3. Short story.   I. Title.   II. Series.
      PR6029.F5Z63   1991
      823'.912—dc20   90-27559

For Carrie, Clare, and Rose

Contents

Contents

PART 3. THE CRITICS

Preface

Liam O'Flaherty was one of the most prolific of major modern writers: he wrote 16 novels, a play, and several books of autobiography, satire, and criticism, as well as the many stories and collections of stories that cemented his reputation. The novels have attracted the most critical attention. Patrick Sheeran, in the longest and certainly one of the most important and useful critical books devoted to O'Flaherty's work, focuses on the novels; John Zneimer, Paul Doyle, and James H. O'Brien all devote far more attention to his novels than to his stories in their respective books on O'Flaherty; and I have written previously about his novels in general and his historical novels in particular.[1]

Despite the critical focus on the novels, most critics agree that O'Flaherty's stories are superior to his novels. Angeline Kelly argues that "as a writer he will ultimately be remembered . . . for his work in the short story"; Diane Tolomeo adds that "O'Flaherty is best known for his stories"; and Brian Cleeve and Anne Brady remark that he "is best known as a short-story writer."[2] Kelly is author of *Liam O'Flaherty the Storyteller*, the only previous book to center on his short stories, and an invaluable source whose bibliography reveals the publishing history of O'Flaherty's stories in English.[3]

My purpose in this book is to offer a fresh critical look at O'Flaherty and his short fiction and to make easily accessible for the first time a wide range of closely related primary and secondary materials, including the largest selection from his letters published to date, that provide insight into O'Flaherty's achievements as a writer. In the case of an author whose life experiences were so diverse and so directly tied to his creative work, an eclectic cultural critique can be particularly rewarding.

In part 1 I explore a series of issues and themes not adequately examined in previous studies. My introduction analyzes the chief tensions running through O'Flaherty's life and work. "Bilingualism" examines his writing in Irish as well as in English, beginning with the fact that the language and culture of his native place, the Aran Islands, were central to his experience and his art. In "Politics" I interpret his

short fiction in the light of his strident socialism and nationalism, especially seeking to explain why his stories seldom appear on the surface
to be openly "political." "Gender" is an attempt to explain O'Flaherty's varied treatment of women, for despite his undeniable misogyny many of O'Flaherty's female characters cannot be reduced to
simple stereotypes. In "Naturalism" I argue that even this most frequently celebrated aspect of his work—transparently evident in his
stories about animal and human life, and death, on the Aran Islands—
turns out to be surprisingly complex, with a strain of romanticism repeatedly countering the naturalism. Another complicating factor, and
one seldom recognized in previous studies of O'Flaherty, is the comic
vein in his work, the focus of "Satire and Comedy." In my conclusion
I emphasize O'Flaherty's overall stature and try to answer the perplex-
ing question of why he stopped writing during the last 30 years of his
life.

Outside of studies devoted to James Joyce, whose work has attracted
more attention than any other modern writer and therefore has been
illuminated by the widest variety of critical perspectives, studies of
Irish authors have tended to be rather conservative, often consisting of
reports on the lives of and simple explications of the works of authors.
Thus, even though O'Flaherty was an avowed Marxist and an obvious
misogynist, no Marxist or feminist analysis of O'Flaherty's work has
appeared. As Robert Scholes writes, "One does not have to be a Marxist to endorse Fredric Jameson's battle cry 'Always historicize!' (the first
words of *The Political Unconscious*)."[4] A crucial part of "historicizing" for
me is understanding O'Flaherty's work in both of his native languages,
Irish and English, which have generally been separated in the study of
Irish literature but are in fact inextricably intertwined, especially in the
case of a bilingual writer such as O'Flaherty.

The thesis I argue links O'Flaherty's peasant status to all my other
concerns: his use of two languages, his politics, his treatment of gender, his naturalism, and his comic and satiric perspectives. It is worth
remembering, however, that while I have separated these topics to
maximize clarity, these issues and themes are thoroughly tied together
in O'Flaherty's work. Naturalism helps to explain O'Flaherty's politics, and vice versa, just as his knowledge of the Irish language helps
to explain his brand of humor.

Instead of trying to mention every story in my critical overview, I
focus on a limited number—yet also on a wide variety of kinds—in
order to suggest the nature of O'Flaherty's achievement. I have made

a conscious effort to choose stories beyond those that have been most frequently anthologized, for the anthology selections have tended to encode just one facet of his work, emphasizing his most clearly naturalistic stories at the expense of other kinds.

That there are other themes and issues in O'Flaherty's life and works, such as his use of folklore and mythology, should be obvious to anyone familiar with O'Flaherty's work. Thus, I have attempted to include a wide range of points of view (including O'Flaherty's own) in the selections reprinted in parts 2 and 3. Collected in part 2 are numerous excerpts from O'Flaherty's unpublished letters and from a number of his essays published in sources that are difficult to obtain. Part 3 consists of selections from some of the best previous O'Flaherty criticism; again I have endeavored to bring together sources that are important but generally hard to find today.

My discussion here is not intended as an attempt at closure, but as an invitation to other new and original interpretations of O'Flaherty. Examining the seamier sides of O'Flaherty, including his relationships with women and his misogyny, has not diminished my admiration for such vivid, masterful stories as "The Cow's Death" and "The Post Office," but has deepened my appreciation for the complexity of his work, warts and all.

I wish to thank a number of institutions and individuals without whom this book would have been impossible (but who should not be held responsible for its errors). I am very grateful for the grants in support of this project that I received from the National Endowment for the Humanities, the Professional Development Council of the Pennsylvania State System of Higher Education, and Indiana University of Pennsylvania. I appreciate the help of my "grantsman," former IUP Associate Dean for Research Gerry Stacy, and offer belated thanks to Lloyd Steffen of Lehigh University for his "classical" assistance. I am thankful to the Harry Ransom Humanities Research Center at the University of Texas, where the O'Flaherty collection is housed—particularly to Cathy Henderson, its research librarian, who was so helpful. In Dublin, I received the assistance of the staffs at the National Library and the Trinity College Library, particularly Eileen Cook at Trinity. I am grateful to the British Library for sending me a copy of the original 1948 text of O'Flaherty's story "Desire" for which I had been searching for several years. The most persistent and crucial library help came to me as always from the staff of the library at Indiana University of Pennsylvania, especially Carol Connell, Janet Clawson, Mary Sampson, David Kauffman, Kathy Redd, and Larry Kroah (library director).

A number of other individuals gave me indispensable help. Pegeen O'Sullivan, O'Flaherty's daughter, kindly gave me permission to quote extensively from her father's letters. O'Flaherty's nephew, the late Breandán Ó hEithir, himself a well-known writer in Ireland, wrote to me generously and helpfully. Professor Tomás de Bhaldraithe of the Royal Irish Academy, probably the world's leading authority on the modern Irish language, kindly read and critiqued "O'Flaherty's Bilingualism," providing me with several corrections and sources I would have otherwise missed. A previous teacher of mine, Professor Alan Harrison of University College, Dublin, sent me one of the texts of a story by Pádraic Ó Conaire that was translated by O'Flaherty. Jane Bolton of Ceiríní Cladaigh in Dublin went to great lengths to obtain and send me their 1978 recording of O'Flaherty, which is no longer in circulation. Several fellow members of the electronic-mail, Irish-language newsgroup GAELIC-L@IRLEARN sent me answers to queries: Marion Gunn (GAELIC-L host), Caoimhín Ó Donnáile (who also uploaded to me a book about Pádraic Ó Conaire), Breandán Ó hAichir, Eoin C. Bairead, Pádraig de Bhaldraithe, and Owen McArdle.

Closer to home, four IUP graduate assistants contributed work to this project, each in succession energetically and conscientiously performing tasks that were tedious and absolutely crucial to the completion of this book: John Tassoni, Dongliang Xu, John D'Ambrosio, and Mark Crilly. A number of other IUP graduate students in two different seminars also contributed to my thinking and writing here: Ross Coombes, Bob Crone, Nancy Johnson, Nancy Lang, Beatrice Lei, Duane Molnar, Mark Noon, Peter Quigley, Amy Scher, Frederic Teillon, Marc Waddell, Judy Washburn, and Andrew Williams. My secretary, Catherine Renwick, handled seemingly endless correspondence and paperwork, often assisted by student worker Daneen Pasinski. Last and most, I offer my undying gratitude to Lea Masiello, who read and critiqued everything I wrote, listened to everything I said, and put up with everything I did.

Notes

1. Patrick F. Sheeran, *The Novels of Liam O'Flaherty: A Study in Romantic Realism* (Atlantic Highlands, N. J.: Humanities Press, 1976); John Zneimer, *The Literary Vision of Liam O'Flaherty* (Syracuse, N. Y.: Syracuse University

Press, 1971); James H. O'Brien, *Liam O'Flaherty* (Lewisburg, Pa.: Bucknell University Press, 1973); and James M. Cahalan, "Liam O'Flaherty's Natural History," in *Great Hatred, Little Room: The Irish Historical Novel* (Syracuse, N. Y.: Syracuse University Press; Dublin: Gill, 1983), 133–53, and "Liam O'Flaherty," in *The Irish Novel: A Critical History* (Boston: Twayne, 1988; Dublin: Gill and Macmillan, 1989), 186–91.

2. Angeline Kelly, "O'Flaherty, Liam," in *Dictionary of Irish Literature*, ed. Robert Hogan (Westport, Conn.: Greenwood Press, 1980), 525; Diane Tolomeo, "Modern Fiction," in *Recent Research on Anglo-Irish Writers*, ed. Richard Finneran (New York: Modern Language Association, 1983), 280; and Brian Cleeve and Anne Brady, *Biographical Dictionary of Irish Writers* (New York: St. Martin's, 1985), 189.

3. Kelly, *Liam O'Flaherty the Storyteller* (London: Macmillan, 1976), 145–49.

4. Robert Scholes, *Textual Power: Literary Theory and the Teaching of English* (New Haven: Yale University Press, 1985), 16. For a fuller statement of this point of view as applied to Irish fiction, see the introduction and conclusion to my *The Irish Novel: A Critical History*, xvii–xxiii, 304–8.

Acknowledgments

I am grateful to the following institutions and individuals:
The Harry Ransom Humanities Research Center and Peters Fraser & Dunlop Group Ltd. for permission to publish quotations from original letters by Liam O'Flaherty to Edward Garnett, in the O'Flaherty Collection at the Harry Ransom Humanities Research Center, University of Texas at Austin.

The editor of the *Irish Press* for permission to reprint "Irish Revival Delights Liam O'Flaherty," 13 May 1946, 4. Copyright 1946 the *Irish Press*.

The Estate of H. E. Bates for permission to publish an excerpt from *The Modern Short Story: A Critical Survey* (Surrey, England: Thomas Nelson, 1941).

Professor A. Norman Jeffares, former editor of *A Review of English Literature*, for permission to reprint excerpts from George Brandon Saul's "A Wild Sowing: The Short Stories of Liam O'Flaherty," 4 (July 1963):108–13.

The editors of *Wascana Review* for permission to quote from Vivian Mercier's "Man against Nature: The Novels of Liam O'Flaherty," 1, no. 2 (1966): 44–45.

The editors of *English Studies* for permission to publish excerpts from Angeline Kelly's "Liam O'Flaherty's Short Stories—Visual and Aural Effects," 55, no. 5 (October 1974): 440–44, 46–47.

The editor of the *Irish Times* and Eoghan Ó hAnluain of the Department of Modern Irish at University College, Dublin, for permission to reprint an excerpt from Mr. Ó hAnluain's "A Writer Who Bolstered the Irish Revival," 8 September 1984, 7.

The editor of *Éire-Ireland: A Journal of Irish Studies*, the Irish American Cultural Institute in St. Paul, Minnesota, and Professor Tomás de Bhaldraithe for permission to reprint excerpts from Mr. de Bhaldraithe's "Liam O'Flaherty—Translator (?)," 3, no. 2 (1968): 149–53.

The editor of *Éire-Ireland*, the Irish American Cultural Institute in St. Paul, Minnesota, and Professor Maureen Murphy for permission to reprint excerpts from Dr. Murphy's "The Double Vision of Liam O'Flaherty," 8, no. 3 (1973): 20–25.

The editor of *Éire-Ireland*, the Irish American Cultural Institute in St. Paul, Minnesota, and Professor William Daniels for permission to reprint excerpts from Mr. Daniels's "Introduction to the Present State of Criticism of Liam O'Flaherty's Collection of Short Stories: *Dúil*," 23, no. 2 (1988): 124–32.

Syracuse University Press for permission to publish an extract from John Zneimer's *The Literary Vision of Liam O'Flaherty*. © 1970 by Syracuse University Press.

Twayne Publishers, a division of G.K. Hall & Co., Boston, and Professor Paul Doyle for permission to reprint excerpts from his *Liam O'Flaherty*. © 1971 by Twayne Publishers.

The editor of *Éire-Ireland* and the Irish American Cultural Institute, St. Paul, Minnesota, for permission to reprint extracts from Helene O'Connor's "Liam O'Flaherty: Literary Ecologist," 7, no. 2 (1972): 47–48, 49–50, 51, 52, 53–54.

Macmillan Press, London, for permission to reprint an extract from *Novelists and Prose Writers*, ed. James Vinson (London: Macmillan, 1979), 927. © 1979 by Macmillan Press.

Lensmen Limited, Dublin, for permission to reproduce the frontispiece photograph of Liam O'Flaherty.

Part 1

THE SHORT FICTION

Introduction:
The Life and the Issues

"You have the characteristics of a low-born Irish peasant. Servile when you must, insolent when you may."[1] Liam O'Flaherty records this allegation in his autobiographical *Shame the Devil* (1934) as coming from the pen of the mother of a young woman with whom he had broken off an engagement in 1923. In the context of a book in which he says that "I have told the truth about myself" (284)—often engaging in Dostoyevskian dialogues with the nagging, alter-ego devil of the title— her accusation is really a self-accusation. He does not bother to deny the indictment, and later in the book he tells an Irish gentleman, "I'm an Irish peasant, and . . . there is a marked difference between us" (174). For O'Flaherty, his status as a peasant was his excuse for doing what he felt he must do in order to survive and succeed.

An awareness of his peasant background is central to understanding not only this author's personality and life, but also his short fiction. That O'Flaherty wrote vividly and unforgettably about rural Irish peasant and animal life has been a critical commonplace for many years. Appreciation of the considerable complexity of his work, however, has often been hindered by the mistaken assumption that behind O'Flaherty's famously "simple" style lay an equally simple view of the world. It is my chief contention in this critical overview that his work and the experiences and convictions so deeply ingrained in it were anything but simple, but rather were marked by a set of interrelated, unresolved, often contradictory tensions and issues.

These conflicts will keep returning us to O'Flaherty's peasant background, so let me begin by sketching the chief facts of O'Flaherty's life. I can offer little more biographical detail than already found in the summaries in earlier books on O'Flaherty; complete command of his life is elusive, at least at this point in time. No biography has been published or to my knowledge even attempted, though I am sure that it is only a matter of time until such a feat is achieved in spite of the obstacles against it. Those obstacles include the lack of any adequate written evidence for a detailed account of O'Flaherty's life after the 1920s until his death in 1984, and especially after the early 1950s when he mostly stopped writing for publication and entered his long later years of relative seclusion. His biographer will also encounter O'Flaherty's scorn for such scholarship. His two most obviously autobiographical books, *Two Years* (1930) and *Shame the Devil* (1934), were written partly in order to steal the thunder of any later would-be biographer who might want to attempt his life.[2] At the end of *Shame the Devil* he asserted, "should I be considered worth a biography, I have robbed grave-robbers of their beastly loot" (284). Moreover, like Seán O'Casey in his autobiographies, O'Flaherty is often misleading. Paul Doyle notes that O'Flaherty was often "deliberately mysterious, vague, and contradictory about many aspects of his life and career."[3] John Broderick stressed in an obituary that O'Flaherty "would never talk about his books" and instead switched the subject, as his nephew Breandán Ó hEithir wrote to me, "to Gaelic football and hurling; subjects that interested him greatly and which he shrewdly surmised would have no interest at all to his interrogators."[4] O'Flaherty himself published a biography, *The Life of Tim Healy* (1927), but it was more a platform for his own ironically expressed views than a straightforward historical study. O'Flaherty's attitude toward biography is suggested in his preface to that book, in which he tells us that when this Irish politician "heard that I was about to write his life," Healy "humorously threatened to write my life in revenge."[5]

At the same time, the younger writer determined to make his way did not hesitate to offer several accounts of his early life on the Aran Islands or his later wanderings in the world before he began to write. Moreover, while O'Flaherty's stories are not generally assessed as directly autobiographical, he did write some that obviously describe and shed light on his own experiences. To mention just a few examples, the well-known "Desire" recaptures an experience of infancy, and "The New Suit," one of boyhood; "The Parting" recounts the adolescent anguish of his departure from his home island for a school on the "mainland" of Ireland. Lesser known sketches and autobiographical essays such as "Christmas Eve," "Fresh Mackerel," and "Village Ne'er-do-Well" describe happy childhood experiences. Such cheerful sketches seem almost surprising coming from the pen of one whose best-known stories (such as "Going into Exile") tend to encode a view of life on the island of Inis Mór as generally harsh and painful.

What are the basic facts of O'Flaherty's life? He was born on Inis Mór on 28 August 1896; he was singled out as a talented young boy who showed promise for a vocation as a priest; he left home in 1908 to study at Rockwell College in County Tipperary and then at Holy Cross College in 1914 and at University College, Dublin, in 1914–15; he fought as an Irish Guard in World War I from 1915 until he was wounded in 1917; he traveled and worked in London, South America, Turkey, Canada, and the United States between 1918 and 1921; he led an ill-fated, short-lived socialist occupation of the government building the Rotunda in Dublin in early 1922; and soon thereafter he began to write, publishing his first works of fiction in 1923.[6] The most biographical and cultural detail about his early life has been provided by Patrick Sheeran, who emphasizes that his family "was one of the poorest of the poor" (18) but was descended from the heroic O'Flaherty clan of western Connacht. Sheeran writes that O'Flaherty did not treat his early impoverished life on Aran "at any length in his autobiographies, partly no doubt for reasons of family pride" (22).

The early years of O'Flaherty's career as a writer were tremendously prolific ones; he published 19 books between 1923 and 1935. This he accomplished in spite of domestic instability: O'Flaherty's letters to his mentor Edward Garnett between 1923 and 1932 were written from a frequently shifting series of addresses in England and Ireland and record his relationships with several women, one of whom he married and separated from during these years. Our knowledge of his life after 1930 is generally sketchy. We know that he apparently spent much of the 1930s and early 1940s in Connecticut, returned to Dublin in 1946, and, after some further wanderings, settled there for the rest of his life. In the early 1950s, after publishing more than 20 books and more than 150 stories selected in more than a half-dozen collections, some of them appearing in his later years but all of them written during earlier years, O'Flaherty stopped writing. He wrote virtually nothing, at least nothing new for publication, during the last 30 years of his life.

It is difficult to overestimate the importance of Edward Garnett (the London writer, editor, and publisher's reader) to O'Flaherty's work, and particularly to his early writings. O'Flaherty himself claimed publicly in 1933 that "I owe Edward Garnett all I know about the craft and a great deal of all I know about the art of writing."[7] Garnett has been mentioned in most of the accounts of O'Flaherty's career; the experience of reading O'Flaherty's more than 150 letters to him demonstrate

Garnett's shaping influence on the Irish writer. Mentor to Conrad, Lawrence, and several other important twentieth-century writers as well, Garnett was crucial not only in advising O'Flaherty about his own writing but also in introducing him to the work of the Russian writers who became so important to him: Turgenev (on whom Garnett had published a book), Chekhov, Dostoyevski, Gorki. Many of their works were originally introduced to the English-speaking world in translations by Constance Garnett, Edward's wife. O'Flaherty was impressed by these writers' treatments of peasant life—particularly in Chekhov, whose story "Peasants" he admired,[8] and Gorki, who was himself a peasant like O'Flaherty.

Thirty years older than O'Flaherty, Garnett served not only as literary mentor but as father figure to him, helping him keep his spirits up and his mind on his writing during often difficult personal trials. O'Flaherty addressed him as "My Dearest Friend" at the beginning of most of his letters after July 1923, and referred to him at one point as "my literary uncle" (24 January 1926). Having noticed his first published story, "The Sniper," in the *New Leader* in January 1923, Garnett had recommended publication of O'Flaherty's first novel, *Thy Neighbour's Wife*, to Jonathan Cape not because he considered it a great novel but because he felt that it was the work of a promising writer. Garnett's admonition to O'Flaherty to write about the Aran Islands (described by H. E. Bates, as reprinted in part 3) recalls Yeats's similar, more celebrated recommendation to Synge, but Garnett's advice was more directly influential on O'Flaherty (who continually recorded his thanks for it in his letters) than that of Yeats to Synge, which was made famous mostly in Yeats's own autobiographical writings.

Of course, O'Flaherty's letters to Garnett are even more important for what they show us about O'Flaherty himself, his view of his world, and his writing than as proof of Garnett's mentorship. Reading all of them creates a more balanced impression than that derived solely from the best-known quotations so frequently cited to demonstrate O'Flaherty's angry, passionate, often arrogant outlook on life and art. Passion and arrogance are indeed characteristic of the man and his letters, but the letters also reveal his desire for approval, his gratitude, his sense of humor, his despair, and his resolve. It is also worth noting that O'Flaherty felt that he had invested more of himself in his novels than in his short stories (which he typically calls "sketches" rather than stories). As illuminating as some of his remarks about his stories are and as persistently as he returned to storywriting, O'Flaherty spent much more time recording his thoughts about his novels *The Black Soul* (1924) and *The Informer* (1925). He clearly wanted most of all to write The Great Irish Novel, and he found solace in the ongoing work of a novel more than in the brief creative outburst of a "sketch." He was frustrated that while his stories were so often praised, his novels were less appreciated, and he feared that his stories often merely followed a formula. But O'Flaherty was wrong; even today most critics feel that his best stories are superior to his 15 novels, which are often flawed— even the best among them, such as *The Informer, Skerrett* (1932), and *Famine* (1937).[9]

O'Flaherty wrote often and at length to Garnett during the period 1923–26; his letters gradually slowed down after that, and there is a gap in the correspondence between 1928 and late February and early March of 1932, when O'Flaherty sent what apparently were his final two letters to Garnett (who died in 1937). He did occasionally record disagreement with his mentor, as when they exchanged a couple of pointed letters about the selection of "The Tent" as the title story of O'Flaherty's second collection of stories, with O'Flaherty defending the story against Garnett's criticisms and admitting that "the fact is that I used it as the title story in the hope that it might sell the book" (24 January 1926).

O'Flaherty maintained an ongoing, very specific interest in the marketing of individual stories to particular journals, peppering his letters with thoughts about which stories could best be sold to particular magazines ("'The Wren's Nest' is no good. We can sell it though," 9 July 1923) and delighting in successful sales ("we can live here for six weeks on 'Red Barbara,'" 12 July 1927). He scorned the reading public in general as "merciless" (12 October 1923)—both the British public ("I have merely to make my living by the British public," April 1924) and the Irish public (with good sales of a book meaning "that about ten copies of it will be sold in Dublin and five in the rest of Ireland," 3 April 1924). He complained that a second-rate story is "the sort of work that the mob likes best. They buy that sort while they reject the first rate" (16 July 1925). In the same letter he adopts a hard-bitten attitude toward reviews, asking upon receiving the proofs of *Spring Sowing*, "Do you think we should expect success this time or further denunciations?" Yet he could positively blush at a favorable review or a good word from an editor, as when he declared that he "got on very well" with Desmond McCarthy (whom he cursed on other occasions) after he agreed to publish "The Black Mare" in the *New Statesman* (20 Au-

gust 1923). A single pointed sentence in the same letter sums up
O'Flaherty's ambivalent, realistic attitude toward editors and the literary marketplace in general: "To hell with them—but one must earn
a living."

O'Flaherty's letters from the period 1924–26 also chronicle his "assault" on the Dublin literary scene during those years, as do his articles
and letters in the *Irish Statesman*, edited by Æ (George Russell). The
most blatant aspect of that self-described personal "campaign" was
O'Flaherty's arrogant ruthlessness in using people for his own
advantage:

> I pat myself on the back. I licked all these swine into a cocked hat.
> When I came here nobody would speak to me. Everybody hated
> me. I wound them all round my fingers. I got Æ to give me a thun-
> dering review. I got all the old women to praise me. Now that I have
> fooled them I am telling these damned intellectuals what I think of
> them in choice scurrilous language. I have gathered a group of faith-
> ful followers about me and am starting a monthly paper called
> *Tomorrow*.
> (Letter to Garnett, 16 May 1924; quoted in Zneimer, 6)

However, *Tomorrow* lasted for only two issues, and while O'Flaherty
enjoyed a number of successes during this period, he also encountered
some hard times and was often more despairing then jubilant. Indeed,
one has to wonder to what extent the most arrogant passages in his
letters reflect a defensive pose designed to mask the pain and isolation
he articulated in letters that have not previously been cited. Earlier he
had admitted his own "unspeakable vanity," adding, "To an intellectual the case around the instrument is not so important as the instrument itself. And to you I hope that Liam O'Flaherty is of absolutely
no importance compared to the artistic soul that sometimes looks beautiful and gaunt within the ridiculous fellow's body" (23 July 1923).
Later he confessed, "I am in a very bad condition here and absolutely
friendless—everybody here has turned against me. I have no money.
Would you ask Cape to purchase the copyright of my four books—for
whatever he can give" (8 January 1925). Garnett responded to this
plaintive plea by sending him money himself, bucking up O'Flaherty
and allowing him to declare defiantly, "I am cast out here. It remains
to be seen who will be cast out last" (29 January 1925).

O'Flaherty remained shell-shocked from his wounding on the western front in 1917, occasionally suffering bouts of bad nerves and depression: "I got a bad nervous stroke on Sunday which kept me prostrate until this afternoon. It's an awful nuisance you know. I can do nothing. I can't think or write or feel cheerful. Afraid to eat anything. All that sort of thing. Chekhov would write a good story about me" (6 February 1924). Indeed, O'Flaherty recorded his own narratives about such difficulties, as reflected in *The Black Soul, Shame the Devil*, and his unpublished story "Terror."[10] O'Flaherty retreated to the Aran Islands on a few occasions during the 1920s in an attempt to overcome his depression and regain his inspiration: "I went down to the Aran Islands for a few days and I was gloriously alive for those days, alone by the sea fishing rockfish. Then I came here again [to Dublin] and I am again as melancholy" (17 June 1927). Like the protagonist of *The Black Soul* as O'Flaherty described him to Garnett, however, he repeatedly found himself "saying to hell with Inverara [Inis Mór]. Civilisation is the thing after all. And he thirsts for Mooney's in Abbey Street and the fellows spitting into the Liffey" (9 July 1923). He was always torn between the simple but difficult natural environment of Inis Mór and the alienating but fascinating spheres of Dublin, London, and New York.

O'Flaherty also vividly recounted his love life to Garnett. In his accounts, O'Flaherty was unabashed, though sometimes afterwards remorseful, about his series of relationships with three women during the years 1923–32: a "Miss Casey" and a "Mrs. Morris" in England and Margaret ("Topsy") Barrington in Dublin, who divorced the historian Edmund Curtis to marry him in 1926 and gave birth to their daughter Pegeen. His ongoing accounts of each relationship reflect in turn his early infatuation or love and eventually his inability or unwillingness to remain living with each woman after the initial spark had gone out of the relationship. After breaking off his engagement to Miss Casey, he lamented, "It is only the things one loves that hurt, *or that one hurts*" (7 July 1923). Just after breaking off with Mrs. Morris and beginning his relationship with his future wife, he wrote, "If a man is a low fellow or a heartless rascal it is mere hypocrisy for him to try and hide the fact of his rascality. . . . I am still a scoundrel in spite of your prediction that I was slowly becoming civilised. The lady who is unfortunate enough to have conceived an affection for me here is also married and lives with her husband very dutifully. . . . She is one of the most sought after beauties in Dublin but she does not enthuse me, at least not very much. But she is good copy" (21 March 1924). Yet a few months after this callous early estimate of his future wife, O'Flaherty declared, "She is just the one woman in the world for me" (4 October 1924). However, his last letter to Garnett several years later reported that "I have separated from my wife and there is talk of my being divorced, but I am not enthusiastic about that as it might put me in danger of remarriage" (3 March 1932).

O'Flaherty's early breakup with Miss Casey returns us to the quotation with which I began this chapter. What was the specific context of that quotation? Early in *Shame the Devil*, O'Flaherty tells how he accepted the invitation of a young woman ("Miss Casey") who had read some of the articles he had written for revolutionary papers to come and stay in her mother's house in London. She "advised me to take up writing as a profession" and "urged me to persevere" after early failures. "She had become attached to me and did not want me to go to America, as I wished to do" (37). After his first novel, *Thy Neighbour's Wife*, was accepted for publication on Garnett's advice, O'Flaherty was jubilant and—"convinced that I was already rich, famous, a man of genius"—asked "Miss Casey" to marry him (42–43). Soon, however, "as my interest in writing as an art increased, the idea of my marriage became more and more repellant," and he left, writing to her "that I was breaking off the engagement" (44). In reply her mother sent him a long letter saying that "I had wormed my way into her house, toyed with the affections of her daughter, ruined her business, and then, as soon as I had found the means of escaping from my penury, I had broken off my engagement in the most offensive manner. 'You have the characteristics of a low-born Irish peasant,' she wrote. 'Servile when you must, insolent when you may.'" There is no denial of this assessment in *Shame the Devil* or in O'Flaherty's letters to Garnett. Indeed, in his letters he recorded his remorse about his treatment of this young woman.

The double-edged nature of O'Flaherty's peasant consciousness— "servile when you must, insolent when you may"—recurs throughout his short fiction, and is the source of its central tensions and contradictions. In brief, what were these conflicts? O'Flaherty abandoned writing in Irish early in his career, in the mid-1920s, but later published a volume of short stories in Irish (*Dúil*, 1953) and declared upon his return to Ireland in 1946 that he favored making Irish compulsory and banning English altogether for ten years.[11] He became notorious in Ireland as the socialist who in 1922 had led a four-day occupation of the Rotunda in Dublin by a group of unemployed men, and his socialism is clear in much of his fiction—yet he often recorded his disdain for politics. He also insisted that he was not interested in style, convinced that writing should be passionate and spontaneous, but his best work is in fact very carefully crafted and research reveals that he revised and rewrote it more than he liked to admit. (It is true that he declared to Garnett, "Damn it man, I have no style. I don't want any style. I refuse to have a style. I have no time for style. I think style is artificial and vulgar" [3 April 1924]. Yet at the same time he frequently mentioned his revisions in letters that have not been given much critical attention, and insisted in another April 1924 letter, "there is a lot of work to be done on those stories yet before they are fit for publication.") His comments in some of his stories and essays are marked by the harshest sexism, but some other stories describe strong or exploited women in ways that appear to counter sexism. O'Flaherty's naturalistic stories about animals and people, often devoid of humor and marked by tragic endings, are well known. Much less well known but significant are the comic stories and satiric essays that he wrote throughout his career, not only relatively late in a more mellow phase as the most widely used, selective anthologies of his work might suggest.

We readers must recognize that we can no more expect consistency of a writer than of any person. The now very old New Critics insisted that we should examine each text on its own terms, not expect different texts to agree, and resist the temptation to "impose" biography and history on literary texts. However, the cultural and historical critic is not so easily satisfied, and is determined to read all texts (whether fictional or nonfictional) in the light of a writer's whole experience. Today in Ireland the word "peasant" is out of fashion—nobody wants to be known as a peasant anymore, one is cautioned in Ireland—but the fact that O'Flaherty repeatedly applied the term to himself, not only calling himself a peasant but dwelling on the implications of what it meant for a writer to be a peasant, has encouraged me in this impression of him. With his many cantankerous contradictions, O'Flaherty embodies a series of dualities still found today among the natives of the Aran Islands: Irish and English, politics versus antipolitics, artlessness yet artfulness, sexism coexisting with strong women, tragedy and comedy—indeed, life and death every day among the animals and people of the islands and the ocean in which they are perched. Let us seek to understand O'Flaherty's conflicts in cultural terms advanced by himself.

O'Flaherty's Bilingualism

To understand O'Flaherty and his work, one must first consider his native place, the island of Inis Mór in the Aran Islands off the west coast of counties Clare and Galway, as well as the language of that place, Irish Gaelic. Like its closest relative Scottish Gaelic, Irish is part of the Celtic family of languages, which also includes Welsh and Breton. At the beginning of the nineteenth century, about half of the Irish people still spoke Irish. By the end of the nineteenth century, when O'Flaherty was born, however, that percentage had dropped to about 15 percent—largely because of the mid-nineteenth-century Great Famine, which included a disproportionately high number of Irish speakers among its victims. Very few of the remaining native Irish speakers could read or write Irish, and no standard written form of the language existed. Spoken Irish persisted as three distinct dialects: Munster (mostly Kerry) Irish, Connacht (mostly Galway) Irish, and Ulster (mostly Donegal) Irish. The prospective writer of Irish faced four difficult obstacles: the lack of any clearly fixed language in which to write, the absence of much of a tradition or a community of writers in modern Irish, a paucity of publishers willing to disseminate Irish writing, and comparatively few readers able to read it. More subjectively, Irish had understandably come to be associated with failure, and to Irish-speaking peasants the wisest course of action for their children seemed to be to leave impoverished Irish-speaking areas and to stop speaking the language as quickly as possible. The grim decline of Irish Gaelic has never been adequately overcome; today, the percentage of people who speak mostly Irish and live in Gaeltacht (Irish-speaking) areas is only about 3 to 5 percent.

However, the language began to receive much better treatment in the late nineteenth century, experiencing a celebrated revival that is still going on. In 1882 the *Irisleabhar na Gaeilge* (*Gaelic Journal*) was begun in Dublin, and in 1893 Douglas Hyde and others founded the Gaelic League. Hyde's collections of Irish poetry and folklore were tremendously influential upon the writers of the Irish Literary Revival. These were often translated into a new, faithful form of Irish English, which John Synge adopted and immortalized in his plays and which helped shape the syntax and diction of many writers, eradicating the old stage-Irish English full of "begorrah," "top of the mornin'," and other words and phrases that Irish people never utter except in self-conscious jest.

Isolated from the mainland by 30 miles of rough Atlantic ocean, the Aran Islands have remained among the most persistently Irish-speaking places in Ireland. But Inis Mór—by far the largest of the three islands and the one that attracts the most English-speaking visitors—witnessed the encroachment of English at a fairly early stage. O'Flaherty's career clearly reflects these general Irish problems and developments. He himself claimed that English was the first language he spoke and that his father forbade the speaking of Irish in the house, though "at the age of seven I revolted against father and forced everybody in the house to speak Irish."[12] His nephew Breandán Ó hEithir, a well-known Irish Gaelic writer himself, notes that O'Flaherty's chief boyhood hero was Dáithí Ó Ceallacháin, the schoolteacher from Limerick who fought for Irish on Inis Mór and without whom Ó hEithir believes the language would have died there. O'Flaherty called Ó Ceallacháin the best man he ever knew.[13] It was a friend of Ó Ceallacháin who arranged for the young O'Flaherty to be able to study at Rockwell College in County Tipperary on scholarship, on the presumption (quite false, as it turned out) that he was cut out for the priesthood.

This meant that O'Flaherty left his native Irish-speaking community at age 13, never to return except for visits. He enlisted in the Irish Guards in World War I as "Bill Ganly." (*Uilliam, Liam* for short, is the Gaelicized form of "William," and Ganly was his mother's maiden name; interestingly, his mother's paternal ancestors had been Protestants from County Antrim.) Obviously, he was thoroughly bilingual from youth—fluent both in Irish and in an English much influenced by Irish—just as Inis Mór as a whole was becoming bilingual, especially as the traffic to and from the island steadily increased. O'Flaherty's English and indeed his narrative techniques retained the mark of his native place, its language, and its rich tradition of oral storytelling. His debt to his mother as recorded in *Shame the Devil* is well known: "Even when there was no food in the house, she would gather us about her at the empty hearth and weave fantastic stories about giants and fairies, or more often the comic adventures of our neighbours" (18). He adds that the "angel of revolt" entered him at the age of nine and he told his mother a fierce fictional tale about how a neighbour had murdered his wife, describing it so graphically that she rushed out to investigate (18–19).

O'Flaherty's attitudes toward and uses of Irish Gaelic were extremely complex. In his personal outlook on the language, as with other cultural concerns, he tended to be a shifting extremist—at some points adamantly in favor of using the language, at others bitterly convinced of the futility of any such attempt. As a schoolboy he won a prize for his writing in Irish; in 1925 he wrote a play in Irish; in 1946 he declared that Irish should be made compulsory; and in 1953 he published a volume of stories in Irish. Yet when he made no money from his play, he bitterly vowed never to write in Irish again, and indeed he continued to write mostly in English and to make his name as a writer in English.

These apparent contradictions return us to O'Flaherty's self-addressed nature as a peasant. For a long time anthropologists such as Conrad Arensberg have examined the tenacious cultural conventions of Irish peasant society; for example, Arensberg described the Irish countryman's willingness to send a wife who did not bear children back to her parents and allow his brother to marry and live on the family farm (in exchange for a "large fortune") so that children could be produced and "the identity of land and family . . . preserved for another generation."[14] O'Flaherty himself devoted a chapter in his *A Tourist's Guide to Ireland* to the Irish peasant, declaring that "Personally, I like him" and lamenting the peasant's oppression by priests, politicians, and gombeenmen. He advised that the tourist will find "decent peasants shiftless, dirty, hungry . . . subservient, fawning, grovelling, terrified of life and death, eager for revenge, envious of success, fickle in their allegiance, unstable in their resolutions, excitable in temperament. . . . The cunning type of peasant . . . rises out of this hellish life, using his cunning and rapacity and his shameless indifference to honour and decency" in order to succeed. On rare occasions the tourist can witness "some brave soul standing up and crying out the gospel of revolt and salvation."[15] O'Flaherty clearly perceived himself alternately as the cunning peasant who succeeded and as the rare, brave, revolutionary soul. As a writer exiled from his native peasant society, he rationalized that he must be a chameleon in order to succeed.

It seems significant not only that O'Flaherty's first public recognition as a writer—his "gold medal" from Philadelphia that "procured a holiday . . . for the whole of Rockwell" ("Gaelic," 348)—was the result of writing in Irish (an essay), but also that it came during his schooldays in the English-speaking world of County Tipperary. The prize obviously made him popular among his schoolmates, and O'Flaherty must have gained an early impression that writing in Irish could be gratifying aesthetically as well as financially. This was an impression that was rudely squashed when he failed to make any money from his 1925 play, *Dorchadas* (Darkness). His early devotion to the language peaked during that year. He wrote to Garnett in July 1925 that he had enjoyed writing his story "Poor People" in Irish first and then promptly translating it into English. Four months later he wrote, "I am now translating my play into English. They are very excited about it in Dublin—the Gaelic crowd. O'Loughlin, who is going to produce it, is exceptionally enthusiastic. I am sending the English version to an agent in London" (21 November 1925).

Concerning writing in Irish, Pádraic Ó Conaire—with whom O'Flaherty had wanted to write his play—emerges as the central mentor as well as object lesson to O'Flaherty. When they first met around 1920, Ó Conaire made a big impression on O'Flaherty with his pipe, his black hat, and his laconic manner. Years later, in 1953, O'Flaherty provided a fairly detailed account of his relationship with Ó Conaire in a memorable article in Irish.[16] They got to know each other in the early 1920s, and Ó Conaire would remain a considerable influence on O'Flaherty. A Galwayman who wrote only in Irish even though it was his second language and offered him few financial rewards, Ó Conaire was the first great prose writer in modern Irish. He championed the Russian novelists, reinforcing in native Irish terms the influence of Garnett.[17] Ó Conaire was an important writer, but he compromised his talent by writing mediocre stories for the Irish public school system in order to survive, and he died in poverty at age 45 in 1928. His life offered lessons not lost on O'Flaherty. In *Shame the Devil* he records Ó Conaire's final visit to him:

> The man looked a dreadful wreck, almost in rags, his body twisted about like an old serf of the soil. Yet his ill-used face still retained some trace of his youthful beauty, and when he gave voice to some fine thought his eyes lit up with the fire of poetry. He seemed to know that death was upon him and to be inspired to a dark rapture by its imminence. The tragedy of his life weighed heavily on him

and he spoke of the evil of his past; but he insisted that he had been driven to the excesses that had made him a homeless wanderer by loneliness, begotten of a lack of recognition.

"No matter what you do," he cried, pointing a finger solemnly at me, "make a home somewhere and stick to it. Have somewhere that you can call your own, even if it's only a mud-walled cabin. That is the important thing. Look at me and take warning. . . ."

He walked the fifty miles into Dublin, where he died two days later.

(156, 157)

The fact that O'Flaherty made little or no money from his play in Irish in 1925 surprised and severely disappointed him, but it would have been old news to Ó Conaire by then. In his 1953 article in Irish, O'Flaherty recounted an anecdote about Ó Conaire in the 1920s that is instructive about both of their personalities as well as entertaining in its own right. When O'Flaherty asked Ó Conaire why he had done nothing on the play that he had agreed to write with him, Ó Conaire told him that he had finished a great novel instead, called *An Fear* (The man), and that he had hidden it in a hole in the ground. Since O'Flaherty insisted on seeing it, Ó Conaire allowed him to dig a huge hole with a crowbar before laughing at him and admitting that there was no such novel. His reply to the younger writer's demand that he explain why he had pulled such a stunt was, "Bhí tú ag éiriú robhunáiteach" (4; You were getting too arrogant). Interestingly, around the same time, in 1924, O'Flaherty published a comic story, "A Pot of Gold," in which the protagonist similarly tricks his friends into digging for a nonexistent pot of gold.

More than 30 years later, O'Flaherty struggled with his own unfinished novel *Corp agus Anam* (Body and soul) for a long time, Breandán Ó hEithir reports, but found writing an extended work in Irish a very hard task and was unable to complete it. Ó hEithir adds that O'Flaherty did not write more in Irish because he had left the Irish-speaking world at age 13, witnessed Ó Conaire's tragedy, and wanted to be as independent as a writer can be (*Willie*, 76). Receiving virtually nothing for his play in Irish, and then a relative fortune for his sensational English novel *The Informer* (published in that same pivotal year of 1925), was truly a learning experience for O'Flaherty. When the Irish enthusiast Una MacClintock Dix complained that O'Flaherty did not write in Irish—thereby repeating earlier complaints made by Pádraic Colum in the *Saturday Review of Literature* and Walter Chambers in the *Irish Statesman*—O'Flaherty's 1927 reply, "Writing in Gaelic," was the most bitter piece of writing he ever published. There he went so far as to say that "I'll take good care not to publish [in Irish] . . . at the mercy of these sows." O'Flaherty's sexism (seen in his use of the word "sows," which may also echo Joyce's famous employment of the word in *Portrait*) was countered by the upper-class bigotry and condescension of his opponents when the genteel Mrs. Dix was assured in a reply by P. J. McDonnell that she "need not feel worried at the attack made upon her by this half-educated, clever savage."[18] For his part, O'Flaherty complained in "Writing in Gaelic" that "I think Colum and other fellows like him are humbugs. If he is interested in Irish and in Ireland why doesn't he stay in Ireland, learn the language and write in it? All the best Irish patriots live in America."

Later, O'Flaherty temporarily became one of those "patriots," returning to the United States (which he had first visited in 1920) to live in Connecticut for several years in the late 1930s and early 1940s. When he came back to Dublin in 1946, he was quoted by the *Irish Press* as advancing very changed views: "I agree wholeheartedly with compulsory Irish, but it is not compulsory enough. As an experiment I should like to see publishing houses confining their activities to Irish. I would go so far as to forbid the speaking of English altogether for ten years. I would make Irish as compulsory as English was in 1848" ("Revival," 4). Visiting the Aran Islands in May of that year, "O'Flaherty told reporters that he advocated horse-whipping or the loss of the right to vote for people who refused to speak Irish and said that when he was a boy at school, an outside child who came to live on the islands had learned to speak the language fluently in three weeks because the other children threw stones at him if he did not."[19] While in the United States he had written some stories in Irish, and following his permanent return to Ireland in 1946 he wrote a few more stories and rewrote some originally composed in English, bringing 18 stories in Irish together in the celebrated 1953 collection *Dúil*. O'Flaherty's "conversion" back to Irish was due in part to his own changed attitudes—reflecting a bit of the same kind of nostalgic patriotism fueled by life in America of which he had earlier accused Colum. Perhaps even more so, it was a response to changed cultural conditions in Ireland that he himself noted in 1946: "I was surprised . . . to find excellent works by writers of Irish. . . . I was delighted to find new writers and new books. There was a first-class new work by a writer named Ó Cadhain."

Back in 1927, Æ had rightly noted that O'Flaherty could not find a publisher in Irish for his frank, uncompromising brand of writing, with the small market in Irish monopolized by "books for schools" (quoted in de Bhaldraithe, *Times*, 10). By 1945 the situation had improved with the founding of the firm of Sáirséal agus Dill, who published *Dúil* as well as Máirtín Ó Cadhain's books. O'Flaherty praised Ó Cadhain's stories in a 1949 review in Irish, lamenting the lack of an adequate readership for his work.[20]

Comparing the angry O'Flaherty of 1927 with the more nostalgic O'Flaherty of the 1950s, we can see how personal and cultural conflicts interact: it was possible for O'Flaherty to respond more positively to the improved cultural situation surrounding the Irish language in the 1950s just as he had felt forced to respond bitterly to the more conservative, financially hopeless predicament in which he and other writers in Irish were trapped in the 1920s. By the late 1940s and early 1950s, O'Flaherty could literally better afford, after the excellent royalties he had earned throughout the 1930s from his books in English (and especially from the film rights to *The Informer*), to publish in Irish.

Most critics have neglected O'Flaherty's thoroughgoing bilingualism and his self-translations. The five previous critical books on O'Flaherty do not adequately treat these aspects of his work or examine his stories in Irish. As Angeline Kelly recognizes, "no detailed study has been made of the effects of O'Flaherty's bilingualism and some useful research remains to be done in this field."[21] In his exemplary study of John Synge's bilingualism, Declan Kiberd laments: "The short stories of Liam O'Flaherty are examined in courses on the Anglo-Irish tradition, with no reference to the fact that many of them were originally written in the native language. Similarly, the Irish-language version of such stories are studied in a separate class, with no attempt to appraise the author's own recreation of these works in English."[22] This last point is reflected by the fact that available criticism in Irish on O'Flaherty's stories in Irish (while generally mentioning his English fiction and influences) do not treat the English versions of these stories.[23]

Chief among the obstacles to achieving anything like a definitive account of O'Flaherty's self-translations is the fact that in most cases we cannot even be sure if a particular story was written first in Irish or in English. A story's publication history is usually the best yardstick; in general O'Flaherty appears to have published first the version of each story in the language in which it was first written. However, this principle does not always hold up; for example, "The Black Mare" was apparently published only in English, but we are as sure as we can be that this story was first composed in Irish, because O'Flaherty indicated to Garnett that "I started out and wrote it in Irish and then translated it into English, using the phraseology that they would use in Aran. . . . I owned the mare myself but I get old Patcheen Saile to tell it; he was the greatest braggart in Aran" (8 May 1923). It is not surprising that O'Flaherty would conceive this story first in the native language of Inis Mór, for "The Black Mare" is a tale directly addressed to the listener/reader in an extremely oral style (more so than in any of O'Flaherty's stories) recounting the death of the narrator's magnificent horse at the end of a race, and filled with proverbial sayings clearly translated from the Irish such as "may the devil swallow me alive" and "I'll swear by Crom that the spell of the Evil One was put on the mare."[24] Scattered through his letters to Garnett are similar proverbial statements, including one recorded both in its Irish original and an English translation: "Mol an óige agus tiucfhadh sí, cáin an aois agus clisfidh sí (Praise youth and it will respond; blame old age and it will fail)" (31 December 1923).

Largely because O'Flaherty himself refused to clarify matters, leaving scholars to try to sort things out for themselves while depending on other sources, the scholarly evidence that has been offered as to which version of a story—Irish or English—was written first is generally inconclusive, often contradictory, and sometimes clearly in error.[25] Further complicating matters is the fact that O'Flaherty often made small but significant changes in different published versions of his stories; one cannot assume that there is a single Irish or a single English version of many of the stories, but rather one might do best to compare and contrast *all* of the available versions of all of the stories in both languages (no mean feat given the difficulty of obtaining copies of many of the periodicals in which they appeared). Indeed, examining different versions of O'Flaherty's stories fairly quickly convinces one that he very often rewrote them. Interestingly, while we can be reasonably certain from the evidence that several stories were written first in Irish ("Daoine Bochta" ["Poor People"], because O'Flaherty himself told Garnett so, as well as "An Buille" ["The Blow"] and "Teangabháil" ["The Touch"], because all of the available evidence agrees) or only in Irish ("An tAonach" [The fair], "An Charraig Dhubh" [The black rock], and "An Fiach" [The hunt], each of which was published only in Irish), there appears to be only one story, "The Cow's Death," which we can be reasonably certain was written first in English before O'Flaherty then translated it for publication in Irish.

Here I wish first to compare and contrast versions in both languages of a story that was certainly written first in Irish ("Daoine Bochta"/"Poor People") with one that was certainly written first in English ("The Cow's Death"/"Bás na Bó"). Then I will offer a close reading of the title story of O'Flaherty's Irish collection, "Dúil" or "Desire"—a story that was especially important to its author—to exemplify how his different Irish-reading and English-reading audiences shaped his writing decisions. Finally, I will discuss some general features of O'Flaherty's bilingual stories and use them as well as the three published only in Irish to comment on O'Flaherty's early life on Inis Mór and his attachment to the Aran way of life. While it is useful to know (in the rare instances when we can) which language O'Flaherty wrote in first in order to compare and contrast his fluctuating processes of self-translation, in another sense it is not crucial to be certain in every case which language he used first, because he did not tend to literally "translate" his own stories. Instead, he rewrote them as he moved from one language to the other, as we shall see specifically in the case of "Dúil" and "Desire."

We can get a clearer picture of O'Flaherty's translations or bilingual rewritings of his own stories by contrasting them to his rendering of a story by his Irish mentor, Pádraic Ó Conaire's "Croidhe-bhrughadh na Cruinne" (The world's heart-pressing), which O'Flaherty translated in 1925 as "The Agony of the World."[26] As Tomás de Bhaldraithe notes, Ó Conaire's title echoes the Irish phrase for the act of contrition in the sacrament of confession, and the story "suggests that the whole world makes an act of contrition for Lucifer's sin."[27] O'Flaherty noted to Garnett that he had sent "a little translation of a beautiful thing by Pádraic Ó Conaire" to Murray at the *Adelphi*, "and he's going to print it" (14 July 1925). Four years later, Cormac Breathnach published a different translation of the same story, entitled "The World's Daily Oblation."[28] The most striking differences between these different versions are in syntax and diction. Breathnach is quite faithful to Ó Conaire's often long, complex sentences, while O'Flaherty rewrites them into his own inimitable style—creating generally shorter, blunt, active sentences and the "passionate" diction for which he always strove. For example, what Breathnach translates quite literally as, "You will say it was the wind blowing through the branches that caused the stir; but I have a different idea as to its cause" (33), O'Flaherty renders less literally (and more effectively) as, "Yes, you say, it was the wind among the branches. But I do not believe it" (258).

Of course, when O'Flaherty translated or rewrote his own stories, he did not need to find ways to remake the dissimilar style of another writer into his own style. Instead, he could follow different choices at various points in order to recreate his own style as he moved from one language to the other. In general, while allowing for the very different vocabulary and idioms found in Irish, the features most celebrated in his English stories can also be found in his Irish ones. In the case of at least one story that we know was written first in Irish, "Daoine Bochta," it is interesting to see how generally faithful, especially in terms of syntax, is his English translation, "Poor People."[29] Both versions grip the reader with a vivid account of the death of a poor couple's young son, belatedly but inevitably discovered by his father on his return home. De Bhaldraithe and Murphy have emphasized the differences between the Irish and English versions of this story, with de Bhaldraithe focusing on phrasing and Murphy on O'Flaherty's minor narrative additions to the English version.[30] But a sentence-by-sentence comparison of "Daoine Bochta" and "Poor People" shows that, in contrast to his translation of Ó Conaire's story, O'Flaherty followed the syntax of his own Irish story very closely indeed when he rewrote it in English, retelling it in virtually the same number of sentences. The method may be explained by a letter to Garnett, written shortly after the original composition and immediate translation of this story, in which he noted that he was stimulated by the experiment of writing it in "Irish first and then translated into English. The whole thing, both the original and the translation, occupied exactly an hour and three quarters. . . . The method was new and therefore sufficiently interesting to excite my energy" (July 1925). Clearly, when O'Flaherty rewrote promptly from Irish into English, he translated his own work quite closely. Any narrative changes and additions in the English version probably came later, as "Poor People" went through at least four published versions between 1925 and 1956.

When O'Flaherty rewrote his famous and favorite story of 1923, "The Cow's Death," in Irish two years later as "Bás na Bó," however, he made many syntactic changes. Both versions tell the unforgettable story of a cow's plunge to her death over a cliff in futile, uncomprehending pursuit of her stillborn calf whose body has been tossed there by her owner. He commented to Garnett in April 1923 that he had written the story "on the lines you told me," calling it "A Cow's Suicide" and sending it to the *Manchester Guardian*; he responded to Garnett's praise of the story and recorded his own pride in it several times in his letters to Garnett throughout the 1920s, including one in which he clarified that "I translated 'The Cow's Death' into Irish and it appeared last week in the organ of the Gaelic League, with a leading article acclaiming it in gorgeous rhetoric the greatest story ever written and the rise of a new poet who would make Irish etc. etc." (July 1925). Comparing the best-known Irish (*Dúil*, 1953) and English (*Stories*, 1956) versions of the story, one finds O'Flaherty cutting both ways syntactically—sometimes lengthening, sometimes shortening—apparently depending on different linguistic and contextual demands. In one case, at the beginning of the story, three English sentences become a single Irish one: "It came from the womb tail first. When its red, unwieldy body dropped on the greensward it was dead. It lay with its head doubled about its neck in a clammy mass" (*Stories*, 9); "Tháinig sé in aghaidh a chos agus luigh sé ar an bhféar glas ina mheall dearg sleamhain, a cheann casta siar ar a dhroim" (*Dúil*, 47). Shortly thereafter, a single English sentence becomes three Irish ones, thereby reversing the syntactic shift: "Then the cow, overcome once more with the pain, moved away from the calf and stood with her head bent low, breathing heavily through her nostrils" (*Stories*, 9); "Chinn an phian ar an mbó ansin. D'imigh sí ón lao. Sheas sí agus a ceann fúithi, a hanál ag teacht go tiubh as a polláirí" (*Dúil*, 47). It appears that when O'Flaherty translated a story later rather than immediately, as in the case of "Daoine Bochta," he rewrote it rather than directly translate it, creating considerably more syntactic variation. It may also be that he found it easier to translate fairly directly from Irish into a version of English that was (in Ireland) much influenced by Irish, than to translate from English into Irish.

A close examination of O'Flaherty's rewritings of "Dúil" and "Desire" during the late 1940s and early 1950s—the high point of his prosperity and the period of his return to writing in Irish after years of bitter abandonment of it—allows us to consider them as free choices. He was able to tinker with his stories—and tinker he did—in order to represent his work and thus, himself, in whatever way he wanted, especially to his Gaelic readership in the volume *Dúil* in 1953 and to his American and world audience in his major 1956 collection *The Stories of Liam O'Flaherty*. The big gap between these two very disparate audiences goes a long way, I believe, toward explaining the subtle but crucial differences, in content more than syntax, between "Dúil" and "Desire."

According to Doyle (133), Delia Ó hEithir said that "Dúil" was written before "Desire," but the story was published first in English in 1948 and, as with many other stories, we probably will never be certain one way or the other. The different choices O'Flaherty made in the two languages are based on separate audiences; those choices are fairly clear regardless of which language he wrote in first. "Dúil" appears to have had a special emotional significance for O'Flaherty. He selected it as the title for his whole volume of stories in Irish (in which he positioned "Dúil" first), and later in life he included it as the sole story in Irish read in the only publicly released recording of his fiction (with O'Flaherty reading it in the matter-of-fact fluent tones of a typical Aran native speaker).[31] The story recounts a baby boy's first vision of the world outside his window; regardless of whether or not we choose to identify this protagonist with O'Flaherty, it seems safe to assume that this vivid episode is in some way drawn from the author's own experience. In telling the infant's little tale, O'Flaherty appears to be revealing something very basic and private about himself. It is striking that the Irish version (*Dúil*, 1953) is tender and thorough; in contrast, the English version (*Stories*, 1956) seems awkward and incomplete. This impression is reinforced by the fact that Pádraic Breatnach praises "Dúil"as so sensitive that "is geall le dea-fhilíocht é" (28; It's almost good poetry), whereas in contrast Angeline Kelly faults "Desire" with the claim that "O'Flaherty has over-rationalised the baby's reactions" (20). In an important sense, these two critics were judging two different stories.

Both the Irish and the English versions of the story are stark and simple. There is no dialogue; the baby boy is presented as an instinctual creature with a great deal in common with the animals of many of O'Flaherty's other stories. The boy is playing near his mother when he drops his rattle and notices beyond it a sunbeam shining in through the window. Fascinated, he watches the sunbeam for awhile, falls down while struggling to crawl to it, tries to hold it in his hand and, frustrated, begins to cry. His mother then picks him up, consoles him, and rocks him to sleep.

All versions, including other published versions in English, contain a considerable number of variants; there are too many of them and they are too crafty to have been random mistakes or arbitrary changes by editors. They indicate that, in contrast to his reputation as a writer

mostly of raw energy and passion—that is to say, no craftsman—
O'Flaherty was in fact an incurable rewriter of his own stories, like his
fellow Irish short-story master, Frank O'Connor. Both were like the
traditional *seanchaí* of Irish folklore, changing the tale with every telling
and for each new audience. O'Flaherty, after all, grew up on Inis Mór
surrounded by such storytellers and prided himself in his youth on already being one of them.

We do well to pay particular attention to what O'Flaherty left out in
the 1956 text of "Desire" that can be found in "Dúil" (1953), for the
1953 Irish text represents O'Flaherty revealing himself to his small
Irish-speaking audience, while the 1956 English text has him showing
his face to the huge English-speaking world. The difference between
the idiomatic Irish and the slightly stilted English follows the same
pattern revealed so astutely by de Bhaldraithe ("Translator") in his
examination of "Teangabháil" and "The Touch." As far as the shift in
style goes, the whole can be suggested by comparing two brief passages
first translated from the Irish, and then in O'Flaherty's own English
rewrite:

> My sharp grief! When he came into the midst of the shining light it
> was clear to his bright eyes that there wasn't anything standing on
> the air. No more were there any tidings on the shining curtain that
> enticed him with the loveliness of the jewels.[32]

> Lo! As he came into the beam of light his startled eyes discovered
> that there was nothing hanging on the air. The shining curtain,
> which had lured him with the beauty of its myriad dancing jewels,
> had vanished.
> (*Stories*, 378–79).

O'Flaherty's English rewrite is certainly more graceful than my own
deliberately literal translation of his Irish, but his use of "Lo!" sounds
as if it had been lifted from *Ivanhoe* or some other old romance. Together with other diction—"myriad dancing jewels"—it suggests (as
de Bhaldraithe hypothesized) that in some sense O'Flaherty was indeed trying to restore the age of chivalry to Aran.[33]

More important, O'Flaherty left out parts of "Dúil" in "Desire," and
these occur at the most important points in the story. The first good-
sized omission comes when the boy, having just fallen down, crawls for
the first time in order to reach the sunbeam: "Now the harsh contact

with the floor did not make him want to scream for help. The jewelled curtain of light, on which his eyes remained fixed, inspired him with such rapture that he paid no heed to the pain. He raised himself on his hands and knees and began to crawl toward the beam. "It was the first time that he had tried to crawl" (*Stories*, 378).

Here is my literal translation from "Dúil":

> Now the sudden contact with the hard floor didn't give him a desire to scream at all. There was such an amount of ease on his heart, from looking at the jewelled curtain with his big dilated eyes, that he took no notice of the pain. He stayed like that in front of the wonder, until his desire increased so much that what his eyes adored was unable to satisfy him. He began envying, between soul and body, to be going together with the loveliness. He lifted himself up on his hands and his knees, with a great expending of desire and strength. He boldly jutted out the lower lip of his open mouth, bravely, and made eagerly for the curtain of light.
>
> He hadn't ever made an attempt before that to crawl.[34]

Notice at least two crucial differences here. First, the Irish version is both more detailed and more heightened, with the boy jutting out his lip "bravely" and making "eagerly" toward the "curtain of light" rather than simply "crawl[ing] toward the beam." Second, it carefully uses a word absent at this point in the English version, *desire—dúil* in the original—in order to emphasize that central theme. In the whole of the Irish text of the story, the word *dúil* or a close synonym (*fonn* or *tnúthán*) is used nine times, but the word *desire* occurs only three times in the English version.

In both versions the sunbeam and the view of the world outside his window put the boy under a spell. In the Irish text, though, the boy falls under a second spell in his mother's arms. The largest omission in the English version occurs just after the crying boy has been retrieved from the floor by his mother: "She dropped her book, ran across the floor, and took him in her arms. He continued to scream in a frenzy of fear as she carried him back to her chair. It was only when she sat down and placed him on her lap and sang as she rocked him gently to and fro that his paroxysm began to lessen. Then she picked up the rattle and shook it once more" (*Stories*, 379). That is all we are told about the mother and the boy's feelings toward her. But in the Irish text we have:

His mother threw from her the book and ran quickly to him. She lifted him up in her arms, kissing him lovingly. He kept screaming while she brought him over to the chair. He didn't calm down until she sat down with him on her lap. When she began humming in a low voice and rocking him gently back and forth, the terror left him and he was quickly silent. She picked up the rattle then from the floor and shook it out in front of him. He gave a little smile 'n laugh and grabbed the noise-making device in his two hands. He began shaking it.

Here beside the womb in which he had taken life he hadn't any regard for the pain or the difficulty of life. Now it was the soft voice of his mother that was putting him under a spell; but this was a quiet and kind allurement. The memory of the distress that he had suffered making a big journey to the door of the world was swept clean away from his mind. An ease and laziness came on him. He stretched out his feet slowly, let out a long sigh and pressed firmly into the warm body of his mother. He began dreaming with his big blue eyes fully open. (my translation)[35]

This fuller, much more interesting description advances a second "spell" or attraction felt by the boy—his instinctual, basic attachment to his mother—balancing it against the enchantment he feels also with the sunbeam and the world outside. Such is a central tension in life: we want adventure but also desire security; we want to wander the globe but we also want to go home to momma. This conflict is deftly suggested and developed in the space of an Irish text that is only five pages long, but it is essentially left out in the English version. In Irish the story ends with a lovely, flowing sentence which in its syntax and cameralike, zooming-out structure, reminds us of Gabriel Conroy's vision at the end of Joyce's "The Dead" (except that O'Flaherty's protagonist intuits life rather than death): "When he closed his eyes at last while falling asleep, he was shaking with desire for another journey out from the womb, through the world behind the shiny curtain, journey after journey, to the end of bodily life, fulfilling the duties of the human race, with fear and sorrow and joy, through the flowery gardens and remote valleys, to the mountain peaks at the base of the sky and up from there, until he'd stand before the eye of God."[36] In the English version we have no mention of a "journey out from the womb" to suggest that attachment to the mother as well as the cyclic movement from the womb to heaven.

Curiously enough, in the 1954 English version of this story in *The Bell*, O'Flaherty did include a briefer variant of the earlier passage in which the boy rocks to sleep beside his mother's breast, and he does refer again to "the womb" at the end—although that version is more stilted and reserved about the boy's emotions of attachment to his mother and does not state that those emotions put him under a second "spell." The earliest published English version (in the London *Evening News* in 1948) includes the same shorter description as in *The Bell* of the boy rocking to sleep with his mother but not the reference to "the womb" at the end."[37]

Can all of these textual differences be dismissed as reflecting merely the foibles of editing? Or was O'Flaherty, writing in Irish in "Dúil" for an intimate Gaelic readership, more comfortable with baring his soul about a basic, vulnerable dependence on the mother? Did he attempt with less success to convey those emotions to a second Irish audience—based in Dublin, reading in English—in *The Bell*, having earlier been even more reserved about them in the London *Evening News*? Why did he feel constrained to delete almost entirely the mother and her womb from the version in *The Stories of Liam O'Flaherty*? Was it perhaps because, feeling more remote from his native place and tinkering with the story for his publisher in New York, the city where he had made his mark many years earlier as a tough Irish exile in the Bowery, O'Flaherty was reluctant to expose himself as fleeing back to his mother? Was the author of the powerful, brutal novel *The Informer* uncomfortable with the prospect of revealing such tender, mother-emotions to the vast English-speaking-and-reading world?

This kind of analysis would need to be applied to each available text of every story in order to identify all the nuances of his rewritings, but perhaps my close reading of "Dúil" and "Desire" suggests the general nature of O'Flaherty's bilingual rewritings for dissimilar audiences. Clearly, his self-translations involve not only the sharp linguistic contrasts between Irish and English but also the social elements bound up with language, including its community and its audience, and the choices about what to say and what to reveal and not reveal about one's very identity.

Writing in Irish, Fiachra Ó Dubhthaigh argues that unfulfilled desire is a central theme not only in "Dúil" but in most of the other stories in O'Flaherty's volume in Irish (23). To close this discussion of O'Flaherty's bilingualism I would like to briefly consider some of those stories—both those that also appeared in English and also the three that were published only in Irish. In "Teangabháil" ("The Touch"), a young woman's attraction to a young laborer is frustrated; she must marry a more secure, older man whom she detests. We have seen how "Daoine Bochta" ("Poor People") focuses on parents forced to watch their young son die—a rude frustration of desire similar to that of the cow in "Bás na Bó" ("The Cow's Death"). A comparable animal story is "An Seabhac" ("The Hawk"), in which a magnificent male hawk dies while trying to save its mate, but the culprits are the men who take his mate from him.

Desire frustrated is not the only theme of the collection; there is also desire promised and fulfilled. "An Culaith Nua" ("The New Suit") recounts a young boy's joy and pride on receiving his first new suit from the tailor. It describes an Aran ritual whose traditional nature (as well as the influence of his older brother on O'Flaherty) echoes through Tom O'Flaherty's book *Aranmen All*.[38] Another happy boyhood story is "An Buille" ("The Blow"), in which a boy gains his father's respect by standing up to him. In "An Scáthán" ("The Mirror") a girl admires for the first time her own naked body as reflected in the water, anticipating the fulfillment of sex and procreation. In "An Chearc Uisce" ("The Water Hen"), two roosters wage combat and then the victor mates with the hen they were fighting over.

In some of the other stories, moreover, defeat and death are depicted not so much as the frustration of desire, but as part of the natural cycles of life and death. In "An Beo" ("Life") an old man dies just as his grandson is born. "An Fiach" (The hunt), one of the stories published only in Irish, vividly describes a dog's pursuit and killing of a rabbit. In another story that appeared only in Irish, "An Charraig Dhubh" (The black rock), the minute forms of animal life on a huge rock in the ocean are described, and then the rock is crushed by a massive wave. Some other stories incorporate humor, satire, or a slightly bemused narrative tone. "Díoltas" ("The Pedlar's Revenge") is a rather macabre tale of a pedlar who tricks his lifelong enemy into eating candles. "Oifig an Phoist" ("The Post Office") is O'Flaherty's best-known comic story, a bilingual and multicultural comedy of errors set in the Irish-speaking Cois Fharraige area of County Galway. The remaining story that was published only in Irish, "An tAonach" (The fair), is the strangest, most unusual story in the collection: an exposition describing exhausted, sweating cattle and people coming down the road to the fair is followed by an uncharacteristic, somewhat stream-of-consciousness narrative exhorting all assembled to "Plaic! Smailc! Tá said ar fad díolta" (130; Eat! Gobble! Everything's sold).

We might expect O'Flaherty's stories (including the many that were published only in English) to reflect both positive and negative views of life on the island, as his own reactions to it throughout his life were multifarious. At one point he wrote to Garnett, "I don't think I exert any judgment whatsoever in my writing at the moment of writing but seem to be impelled by the Aran Islanders themselves who cry out dumbly to me to give expression to them" (31 July 1925). At other points, however, we can sense him agreeing with the protagonist of *The Black Soul*, who (as he told Garnett) "finished up by saying to hell with Inverara" (9 July 1923). Yet only four years before his death, he visited his birthplace near Gort na gCapall and noticed "a rock which he recognized from his childhood and addressed it affectionately, 'Bail ó Dhia ort, a chloc mhór, tá aithne agam ortsa' [God bless you, big rock, I remember you]. Every stone, field, and hillock was impressed on his memory" ("Death," 1).

Politics

O'Flaherty's politics were no less complicated or polymorphous than his bilingual career. More than once he contradicted himself on the question of whether the writer should incorporate a political stance in works of fiction. On the one hand, he declared in *Shame the Devil* that "it is more necessary for a creative writer to know political economy than for a painter to have eyesight. The writer who remains indifferent to the social movements of his time, or fails to understand them, could never write anything of value. A writer of the present day must be a Marxian, a worshipper of the machine, for Marxism and the machine are the power and the explanation of our era" (31–32). He added that "the strongest driving force of our times is the driving force of the revolutionary proletariat" (197): "Throw away your pansies, slim aesthetes, and carry the wild rose of insurrection" (205). On the other hand, reviewing Sinclair Lewis in 1924, O'Flaherty insisted: "Novels would be far more interesting and far more artistic if novelists merely described life instead of trying to change it according to their ideas. Because a novelist, as a rule, if he is a good novelist, is a little less intelligent than a policeman when it is a matter of telling people what is the matter with America, or what is the matter with Ireland. The business of the novelist is telling us how Americans live, manipulate oil stock and chew gum, or how Irishmen die for their country. No comments are necessary."[39] Two months later he exclaimed, "Would that we Irish could exchange a whole shipload of our political martyrs for a genius like Guy de Maupassant."[40] The fact that such views were not limited to O'Flaherty's youth is underscored by Frank O'Connor's 1956 review of O'Flaherty in the *New York Times Book Review*, in which he reports O'Flaherty's insistence to him that the real writer is simply the one who "can describe a hen crossing the road."

O'Flaherty both expressed and publicly demonstrated his devotion to socialism, yet he also frequently registered his disdain for politics. The most dramatic and best-known public enactment of his socialist beliefs was his leadership of a four-day occupation of the Rotunda in Dublin in January 1922 to protest the unemployment of 30,000 Irish citizens. For this act he was long remembered, and the headline of the *Irish Times* obituary (more than 60 years later) read: "The man from Aran who hoisted the red flag over the Rotunda."[41] Less than two years after the Rotunda occupation, however, O'Flaherty admitted to Garnett that "I can hardly remain of the same opinion on any political matter for more than a week at a time" (22 November 1923). A few years later he wrote in *Two Years* (1930), "By nature I find real pleasure only in thought and in the observation of life . . . I have never performed any social act except on the spur of necessity."[42] In his 1926 article "Fascism or Communism?" he expressed the belief that Ireland was unsuited to either form of government—with a large peasantry "more subtle, more cunning" than the small proletariat—and would have to invent some other political structure.[43] In *The Life of Tim Healy* (1927), he claimed that "I know nothing about politics and care less," explaining that "I became a patriot merely in jest; a form of patriotism which is the only one permitted in Ireland" (6, 7). One result of his patriotism "in jest" was his 1931 pamphlet *A Cure for Unemployment*, wherein he advanced a Swiftian proposal that the unemployed be adopted as house pets.[44] He noted in *Tim Healy* that "in Ireland the politicians are universally regarded with suspicion. We are undoubtedly a very intelligent people" (66). His satiric book *A Tourist's Guide to Ireland* (1929) includes scathing chapters on politicians, priests, and publicans; he emphasized there his belief that Ireland is dominated even more by priests than by politicians (in a country in which religion is a highly political institution). He declared in *I Went to Russia* (1931) that "Bolshevism means no more to me than Lord Beaverbrook's Empire Crusade or the Roman Catholic Religion. I loathe all political beliefs."[45]

These are not merely isolated declarations. A brief synopsis of O'Flaherty's "political career" underscores both the depth and the variability of his beliefs and actions. Just as he inherited his storytelling abilities from his mother, he acquired his politics largely from his father. As James H. O'Brien notes, his father was "a Fenian and a Land Leaguer who apparently forgot at times his obligations to his large family. An incurable rebel, the older O'Flaherty harassed the land-grabbers on Aran and was the first *Sinn Feiner* on the island" (16). Like the famous union and Easter Rising leader James Connolly, whose book *Labour in Irish History* (1910) influenced him,[46] O'Flaherty closely linked socialism and nationalism. His own first public political act was joining the nationalist Irish Volunteers while he was a student at

University College, Dublin, in 1913 ("Death," 1). He later recounted in *Shame the Devil* how, around the same time that he joined the Volunteers, he sat in the National Library eagerly reading *Das Kapital* for the first time: "I attended no more lectures, but I spent ten hours in the library each day for a fortnight studying Marx" (31). Yet in the very next year, when many other idealistic young Irishmen were joining Connolly's Citizen Army or the Volunteers and preparing for the jointly nationalist and socialist Easter Rising of 1916, O'Flaherty enlisted in the Irish Guards of the British army, serving in World War I until he was wounded in France the following year. He admitted in *Two Years* that the Easter Rising, "even though it was led by Connolly, one of the most profound of socialist thinkers, did not make any impression on me" (70), though "the Russian Revolution of 1917 . . . made a profound impression on me" (71). But, like many other Irish people who were indifferent or even hostile to the Easter Rising in 1916, O'Flaherty became strongly nostalgic about it later, attacking Seán O'Casey's socialist critique of it in his play *The Plough and the Stars* because he felt that it did not do justice to Connolly, Pádraig Pearse, and its other leaders.

Ironically, it was while serving in World War I that O'Flaherty came in even closer contact with socialist ideas through association with his fellow soldiers. Though injured and shell-shocked, he remained grateful to the army for having brought him out of himself as a person. He later even published a nostalgic article about his army days and in praise of professional soldiers entitled "Good Soldiers Play Safe."[47] Frequently recording during his career a scathing rejection of pacifism, he went so far as to refer in *Shame the Devil* to "you damned pacifists" and to assert that "to my mind it would be a good thing in life that all individuals who could not be trained into guardsman should become corpses" or at the very least be banned from government (238–39).

Following his discharge in 1918, O'Flaherty joined some socialist societies in London, took part in the James Connolly Society in Boston when visiting his brother Tom in 1920, and was one of the founders of the Irish Communist party after the Treaty of Partition of 1921 (which divided Northern Ireland from the Republic of Ireland). As late as 1940, he expressed the opinion that the partition of Northern Ireland from the Republic of Ireland was maintained by class interests, and believed (naively, as it turned out) that "if there were a labour government in England it would not maintain the partition for three hours."[48] In 1921 "when trade unionists were occupying four mills, bakeries, mines and factories in Cork, Mallow, and Limerick . . . O'Flaherty thought the social revolution was coming" ("Death," 1). His obituary notice described his short-lived occupation of the Rotunda in January 1922, and pointed out that this dramatic political act turned out to be an anomoly in O'Flaherty's life: "'We are holding this place as a military operation and the men are under strict military discipline,' he told reporters who noted that he was styled commander-in-chief and was saluted by his supporters. . . . That was virtually the end of his active political career, though he briefly joined Rory O'Connor and the IRA in the Four Courts in June, 1922."[49]

In *Shame the Devil* O'Flaherty remembered overhearing an old woman in Dublin a few days after the Rotunda episode asking her friend, "Did ye hear that bloody murderer, Liam O'Flaherty, is killed, thanks be to God?" (35). "Ever since then, I have remained, in the eyes of the vast majority of Irish men and women, a public menace to faith, morals and property, a Communist, an atheist, a scoundrel of the worst type. . . . Crave forgiveness? Clip the wings of my fancies, in order to win the favour of the mob? To have property and be esteemed? Better to be devoured by the darkness than to be haunted by dolts into an inferior light" (22, 23). The tone of this recollection suggests that O'Flaherty became embittered by the result of his public political activity and turned to writing partly as a refuge from it. His career as a writer began shortly thereafter when he began writing fiction and revolutionary articles at the home of "Miss Casey," until he was cast out by her mother.

Regarding the Irish peasant, O'Flaherty recorded the opinion in *A Tourist's Guide to Ireland* that "he is in process of transformation, and goodness only knows where he may get to and what he may become. Personally, I like him, and he is the only natural type of human being in this country that I consider an honour to the country and to mankind. As he forms ninety per cent of the community, it will be seen that I consider the Irish race a very fine race. But, like a mangy dog, the peasant needs a good and continuous treatment with some stringent sort of medicine in order to rid him of all the parasites I have named in preceding chapters" (109)—the priests, politicians, and publicans.

Under closer inspection, we can see that O'Flaherty's combination of a devotion to socialism with a disdain for politics represents less a clear contradiction than a subtle tension with an explanation. In fact, he explained himself explicitly in *Tim Healy:* "If a politician has polit-

ical convictions he is not a politician. He is that dangerous social phe-
nomenon called an idealist. He insists on propagating his political
idea when nobody wishes to listen to him," whereas "the good politician . . . has no political convictions. He merely follows the wishes of
the mass of the community at a safe distance" (250). Having been
driven from the Rotunda in 1922, O'Flaherty obviously saw himself as
an idealist, maintaining a determined, often noisy, but fairly hopeless
attachment to socialism while increasingly dedicating himself to his
writing. One of the few other times that he felt part of an intellectual
and political group was in 1924 when he founded and edited two issues
of the newspaper *Tomorrow*, which he described to Garnett as "a platform for myself" (16 May 1924), having earlier referred to his plans to
become well known in Dublin cultural circles as "my political campaign" (20 August 1923). *Tomorrow*, however, quickly folded, and by
early 1925 O'Flaherty felt that he was an outcast in the Dublin cultural
world. He was renegade enough to criticize Soviet society in *I Went to
Russia*, written as he confesses at the outset because "I had to scavenge
among the Bolsheviks or starve a little later" (10), but in *Shame the
Devil* he recorded a rare apology, noting that he regretted the "criminal
mockery" (as he put it) contained in *I Went to Russia* (135).

While about half of O'Flaherty's novels deal extensively with the
public Irish political world—including his most famous novel, *The Informer*, about the IRA in the early 1920s, and his best one, *Famine*,
which contains not only graphic depictions of rural life and poverty but
also occasional socialist editorializing—his short stories rarely treat public politics directly. His public politics seem to have been largely omit-
ted from his stories, at least on the surface. Only about a half-dozen of
his more than 150 published stories focus on Irish warfare or public
political struggle. However, many of his stories are political in a
broader, much more basic sense. They reflect O'Flaherty's continual
interest in how people are controlled by political forces including not
only soldiers and politicians but also priests, landlords, economics, and
the surrounding community. Nonetheless, the question of why he
wrote so infrequently about warfare and public political conflict in his
stories, while very often focusing on these subjects in his novels,
should be addressed. Part of the reason may lie in the commonsense
explanation that O'Flaherty probably felt that the novel provided a
broader canvas for large-scale events such as wars and other major historical phenomena, whereas short stories were better suited for smaller-
scale occurrences.

Additionally, from the beginning O'Flaherty wrote his stories under the strongly modernist influence of Garnett, with an ethos that stressed T. S. Eliot's notion of the "objective correlative" and James Joyce's insistence that the artist should be "like the god of creation . . . invisible, refined out of existence, indifferent, paring his fingernails."[50] Like F. R. Leavis and I. A. Richards, Garnett was an English precursor of the later American New Critics in ways effectively critiqued (in the case of Leavis and Richards) by Terry Eagleton.[51] Another "discovery" of Garnett—the Polish émigré Joseph Conrad, whose work was greatly admired by O'Flaherty and provided the subject of the only pamphlet of literary criticism he ever published[52]—wrote to Garnett, "There are things that I *must* leave out."[53] Clearly learning this modernist lesson well, O'Flaherty expressed to Garnett a similar opinion: "I feel that 'what is good in itself' should be better than what is good largely by artifice. . . . The harder the rock the longer it lasts. . . . The modern short story or sketch seems to have become a poem and where ideas and images attain lordship over poetry it ceases to be elemental and universal" (17 June 1927). Politically O'Flaherty remained a nationalist and a socialist, but because of Garnett's strong influence his code as a short-story author was modernist and he became a master of the art of omission.

This literary code did not leave much room for public politics in short fictional works. John Zneimer writes that "in all of O'Flaherty's letters to Garnett from 1923 until 1932 there is not one mention of communism, socialism, or other concerns about the organization of society. Garnett directed himself to O'Flaherty the artist" (48). Zneimer exaggerates; O'Flaherty did, for example, note delightedly to Garnett on 14 March 1924 that the Dublin proletariat still remembered him for the Rotunda incident, and complained about being rejected as a Communist on a couple of occasions. But it is true that in these letters O'Flaherty mostly ignored public politics in favor of his extensive attention to his writing and personal life. At one point he wrote, "I feel that my philosophy of life is changing or has changed since the birth of my daughter. I feel very conservative or rather revolutionary conservative" (15 May 1926). In *Two Years* O'Flaherty remarked that socialists are "the most conservative people in the world. Notice how they never even change the colour of their neckties" (312).

The influence of the genteel Bloomsburyman Garnett on O'Flaherty was not only literary but also personal and class-oriented. O'Flaherty's penultimate letter to him on 29 February 1932 is typical and summarizes the deferential tenor of his correspondence in this respect: "Permit me to thank you once again for all you have done for me and for the joy your existence gives me—you who are the one person in this dismal age of charlatans that makes literature appear a profession worthy of a gentleman. Please believe me when I say that I am your most humble servant." Throughout their correspondence he always referred to Garnett's mistress as "Miss Heath," never by her first name. Even in his political writings O'Flaherty sometimes showed a tendency (shared by many Irish people) to worship, not a fellow peasant such as the Land League founder Michael Davitt, but instead the upper-class nationalist lords such as Charles Stewart Parnell and Éamon de Valera; he noted in 1936 that while his own socialism and support of the U.S.S.R. was certainly not shared by de Valera, "any Irishman who fails to appreciate the magnificent work being done by President de Valera is an enemy of his country."[54] A comment such as this reveals the other side of O'Flaherty the peasant. Politically he was frequently "insolent"—an angry socialist and nationalist—but with someone such as his literary mentor Garnett, who guided him to success and gave him money and gifts, he was quite "servile," and he learned his modernist lesson very well.

However, O'Flaherty's first published story, "The Sniper" (1923), which (along with the manuscript of *Thy Neighbour's Wife*) initially brought him to Garnett's attention, is one of the handful of his stories set amidst warfare, the most obviously political of topics. "The Sniper" vividly describes a Republican gunman's shooting of a Free Stater foe; its final sentence—within the context of the bitterly divisive civil war in which Republicans fought unsuccessfully for a united Ireland against Free Staters who had accepted partition as a necessary compromise— is startling but credible: "Then the sniper turned over the dead body and looked into his brother's face" (*Short Stories*, 61). "Civil War" (1925), also set in Dublin, turns the tables by showing how a quiet Republican soldier dies just as surely as his deranged compatriot (and just as surely as the Free Stater victim in "The Sniper"), in a brutal war that respects no distinctions. O'Flaherty interjects no editorial remarks in these stories, letting events speak for themselves as in his animal stories in which one beast mercilessly hunts another. An animalistic strain is even stronger in "The Alien Skull" (1929), a World War I story that describes an Irish soldier's fatal experiences in such a way as to undercut O'Flaherty's expressed nostalgia about his army experiences. Considering his pathetic, pained letters to Garnett that describe his long-term neurasthenic shell-shock, one might surmise that the nostalgia and promilitaristic bluster found in those articles reflected a public pose in conflict with O'Flaherty's true private attitude. Similarly, close consideration of "The Terrorist" (1926), which focuses on a demented would-be bomber in a Dublin theater (who calls to mind Gypo Nolan of *The Informer*), might lead one to see this story as O'Flaherty's depiction of the other, darker side of political protest.

In "The Mountain Tavern" (1927) Free Staters bomb and attack a rural Republican hideout, with O'Flaherty employing imagery and syntax that recall Joyce's "The Dead": "Night fell and snow fell, fell like soft soothing white flower petals on the black ruin and on the black spot where the corpse had lain" (*Cormorant*, 120). "Blackmail" (1926) depicts the carryover of the sordid Civil War atmosphere into postwar politics: one Free Stater blackmails another over an earlier secret killing; the politician pays off his blackmailer and starts thinking about how he will get rid of him. A fairly similar story is "A Public Scandal" (1925), in which a newspaper editor cancels his plan to publish an editorial condemning a violent politician when he learns that the politician has just paid a large sum for advertising in the paper. Analogous is "Offerings" (1926), in which a priest pockets the money that people bring to the wake for the four-year-old daughter of poor parishioners.

O'Flaherty published several stories of this kind in which priests are characterized as just as bad as, or worse than, any corrupt politician. He was arguably the most anticlerical writer in modern Irish literature. In *Two Years* he stressed that "I never could see any difference between a man being a pimp and being pope" (61). His sharply satiric chapter on priests in *A Tourist's Guide to Ireland* ranks them as even more powerful than politicians. He advises the newcomer to a parish to take up residence in the bed-and-breakfast owned by the parish priest, get on his good side with the right kind of talk and vague promises of large donations to the church, and then leave town before the payoff. "The parish priest has a finger in every pie. He is the great and only power in the district" (19). Like the nineteenth-century Irish writer William Carleton, O'Flaherty had studied for the priesthood and then subsequently rejected Catholicism and wrote several caustic stories about priests and the priesthood. Benedict Kiely claimed that "O'Flaherty himself, like a very large number of young Irishmen, was for awhile the gesturing patriot and might easily have developed into the menacing priest."[55] Only many years later, in "The Parting" (1948), was he able to render the experience of his own painful departure from Inis

Mór to study for the priesthood. "Benedicamus Domino" (1924)—one of the stories that he told Garnett (16 May 1924) would hurt sales in Ireland of his first volume of stories, *Spring Sowing* (1924)—sardonically portrayed the foibles and infidelities of the brothers in a monastery school like the one where O'Flaherty had studied in County Limerick.

Like "Offerings," his other stories about priests are especially biting. For example, "The Outcast" (1925) vividly narrates a priest's harsh, puritanical rejection of a young unmarried woman who has just had a baby, comes to him for help, and then commits suicide with her baby after he banishes her. O'Flaherty's best-known story about a villainous priest, and one of the best among all of his works, is "The Fairy Goose" (1926). As O'Brien notes, this story "may not compress all the history of religion as Frank O'Connor once said, but it again utilizes the simple, permanent world of peasants to dramatize a cycle of a religious belief" (114). It draws strength from folklore, satire, and tragedy: people believe that old Mary Wiggins's goose brings them good luck until the parish priest puts his curse on it, and then they stone it to death. Christianity thus brutally vanquishes paganism, but what we remember is Mary Wiggins's own memorable curse and O'Flaherty's dismissive moral: "It is certain that from that day the natives of that village are quarrelsome drunkards, who fear God but do not love one another" (*Cormorant*, 129).

Just as charged with O'Flaherty's particular politics are his stories delineating Irish poverty and degradation, both urban and rural. "Wolf Lanigan's Death" (1924)—which O'Flaherty described to Garnett as "a damn sight more *Russian* than either *The Black Soul* or 'The Doctor's Visit'" (April 1924)—appears to be a practice piece for *The Informer*, for it portrays a down-and-out man in Dublin who has killed a policeman and is fated to die violently. "A Dublin Eviction" (1924) reads like a wishful redaction of O'Flaherty's role in the Rotunda in 1922: after bailiffs evict a family, an angry Dubliner leads an impromptu "Irish Workers' Red Army" in a counterattack that results in the restoration of the tenants to their dwellings. The later, rural story "The Eviction" (1948) is a bleaker, rather Gothic tale—recalling both Maria Edgeworth's *Castle Rackrent* and Robert Browning's "My Last Duchess"—in which the ambitious peasant Festus Lynch enacts revenge on the declining landlords who had earlier evicted his own family by taking over their estate, particularly gloating over his acquisition of the painting of their ancestor on the wall. O'Flaherty's stories of rural poverty, like "Daoine Bochta" or "Poor People," are grim in tone and exacting in style and characterization.

One of his greatest stories is "Going into Exile" (1924), in which he unforgettably narrates the "American wake" held for a family's oldest daughter and son who are forced to leave their native island to work in Boston, at a time when such a departure meant that their parents would probably never see them again. Vividly depicted are the repressed emotions of both parents and children, with the mother finally breaking into a lament just as her children leave the house after the all-night wake: "She burst into wild tears, wailing: 'My children, oh, my children, far over the sea you will be carried from me, your mother' . . . 'Come back,' she screamed, 'come back to me.' She looked wildly down the road with dilated nostrils, her bosom heaving" (*Cormorant*, 64, 65). O'Flaherty wrote here directly from his own experience: several of his older siblings had either died or emigrated from Inis Mór by the time he was born as the eighth of nine children. The mother's elemental grief in this story recalls the instinctual reaction of the cow in "The Cow's Death" (1923), compared therein to a mother's anguish.

Just as O'Flaherty was encouraged by the success of "The Cow's Death" to write more naturalistic stories about animals, the triumph of "Going into Exile" stimulated him to write further stories about the people of Inis Mór, increasingly examining the social and economic subtleties of their world as his career progressed. He mentioned to Garnett that "I have had letters from every publisher in Dublin asking for a collection of short stories after the publication of 'Going into Exile' in the *Dublin Magazine*" (2 May 1924).

Two stories illustrate the ability of Aran peasants to bargain and succeed within the sharp confines of the island economy, for such comparatively good fortune was just as much a part of island life and O'Flaherty's political ethos as were poverty and repressive priests. These stories appear to both praise and criticize peasants' modest financial successes, reflecting O'Flaherty's deep ambivalence about peasant life. In "Two Lovely Beasts" (1946) Colm Derrane is driven by socioeconomic hubris: he buys poor Mrs. Higgins's calf, thereby breaking "God's law" by owning *two* bullocks, and by the end of the story is planning to open a shop. O'Flaherty had demonstrated at greater length in *Famine* (1937) that he considered shopkeepers to be the ultimate petty-bourgeois rogues. O'Brien sagely notes that this story "might be interpreted as a fable on the origins of capitalism" (112). Indeed, many of the strong majority of O'Flaherty's stories that do not appear to be directly about "politics," even perhaps some of his animal stories, could be read politically in useful ways. The earlier "Selling Pigs" (1924) combines characterization of the tender relationship of a recently married peasant couple, like those found in such stories as "Spring Sowing" and "Milking Time," with an account of how they craftily entertain and bargain with a "jobber" who buys their pigs. O'Flaherty implied in his 2 May 1924 letter to Garnett that he preferred "The Rockfish"—a sketch of animal life, free of dialogue and objectively "correlative" in the modernist mode emphasized by his mentor—to "Selling Pigs," but one has to suspect that he knew that "Selling Pigs" was a very good story of the kind that he was uniquely qualified to write. A story such as this is just as crucial to an appreciation of its author's politics as a more obviously political story like "The Sniper," and indeed his politics permeate all of his works, not only the stories and other writings mentioned in this chapter. As Terry Eagleton stresses in *Literary Theory: An Introduction*, all writing is political, not just that which openly announces itself as political—a point well worth holding in mind as one reads O'Flaherty's stories.

Gender

Two recent and insightful books on gender and major male modernist writers are Sandra Gilbert and Susan Gubar's *The War of the Words* and Declan Kiberd's *Men and Feminism in Modern Literature*.[56] Both books are of special interest in exploring gender roles in O'Flaherty's works because Gilbert and Gubar have established themselves as leading feminist critics, while Kiberd, writing as a male feminist, is Irish and gives special attention to Yeats and Joyce (though he never mentions O'Flaherty). Gilbert and Gubar focus on the misogynist proclivities found in male modernists; Kiberd, on androgynous impulses. For example, Gilbert and Gubar highlight Joyce's derisive parody in the "Nausicaa" chapter of *Ulysses* of what he described as the "namby pamby marmalady drawersy style" of female romances (146), whereas Kiberd concentrates on Leopold Bloom's many androgynous tendencies, seeing them as rooted in Joyce's own affirmation of the feminine within himself (171–203). Both views are valid, and their contradictory nature points to the many ways of reading Joyce as well as to the fact that gender is an issue fraught with many tensions and contradictions.

Moreover, these polar views allow us to envision a spectrum running from misogyny to androgyny, against which to measure a writer such as O'Flaherty. Was he more misogynist or androgynous, more disdainful of women or sympathetic to them? The quick answer is that misogyny is by far the stronger current that runs fairly obviously through his letters and essays, in particular, and through some of his stories. He often viewed women in the most sexist terms, as erotic and procreative objects for men. Though they do not mention him, Gilbert and Gubar would have a much easier time fitting O'Flaherty into their critique of misogynist male modernists than Kiberd would into his celebration of androgyny. But O'Flaherty did register occasional guilt about his poor treatment of women, and he did write several stories that center sympathetically on women victimized by men and on strong female protagonists. My challenge here will be to explain such stories in light of their author's blatantly recorded misogyny.[57]

In *Shame the Devil* O'Flaherty advances a portrait of the artist that suggests androgyny—or hermaphroditism—at first but then quickly explodes with misogynist, highly stereotyped versions of gender: "A creative artist is half man and half woman. The woman in him is always craving for luxury and public esteem, holding up her child for admiration, longing for the position of honour at a public banquet. But the man in him, the possessor of the seed, becomes corrupt and impotent under the influence of wealth and flattery. And for that reason he must always hold the woman on the flat of her back" (103). O'Flaherty meant this as a confession of his own predilection for popular success and praise, for good reviews and sales, but his presentation of it as a feminine trait that should be repressed and abused (rather than as a clear function of the male ego) is twisted and offensive. On more than one occasion he expressed his male ideal of creative passion and violence—art as something contained in "the seed," and fiction as "a relentless picture of life, as lashing in its cruelty as the whip of Christ when there are moneychangers to be beaten from the Temple."[58]

Yet O'Flaherty was also his mother's son, and he knew it. He inherited her storytelling abilities, and he enlisted in the British army under her maiden name. In *Two Years* he recounted visiting her grave, feeling "as if a knife were thrust into my bosom" (16) and realizing that "her life was a tale of hardship and misery, an endless struggle to find food for her many children. And yet how gay she was in spite of all her sufferings!" (17–18). He indicated to Garnett his opinion that "women hand down the characteristics of genius, the waywardness of the mind" (May 1923). In a comment that underscores his deep ambivalence about gender, he referred to "the cliff-bound shores of Aran" in *Two Years* as "the school in which we, as boys, were taught our manhood; and it was the school also, where I especially was taught by my mother to appreciate the beauty of nature" (75). Elsewhere he noted that "she used to knit and teach me to listen to the singing of larks and to the warbling of blackbirds, and to understand the movements of insects in the grass. She told me that everything that moved or sang was beautiful and had been created by God."[59] A rough, tough code of "manhood," but also a deep and feminine-influenced appreciation of "the beauty of nature"—these were two sides of O'Flaherty's personality, and they are also two central aspects of his stories. His recognition that life on Aran was his "school" returns us yet again to his motto about himself as a peasant both "servile" (stereotyped as a female behavioral trait) and "insolent" (typecast as male). In this respect, Gearóid Denvir's remark about the work of oral Irish-language poets today in the neighboring region of Connemara seems apt: "Much traditional literature can at times be rather anti-woman (if not downright misogynist!). . . . Their conservatism is . . . strongly to the fore in their attitudes to . . . the role of man and woman."[60] The Marxist O'Flaherty was much more radical about social and political issues than these poets, but he shared their outlook on gender. Though he could rid himself of the traditional views of church, state, and class that he absorbed growing up on Inis Mór, sexism was so bred into him by his rural Irish socialization process that he never openly challenged this part of his belief system.

There are many instances of clearly expressed misogyny in O'Flaherty's private letters and public essays. To Garnett he declared that "a woman is not necessary to my life" (April 1923), that "all women I have ever lived with were a curse" (30 May 1923), that one of D. H. Lawrence's books "I have heard . . . condemned by a bitch of a woman so it must be good" (8 May 1923), and that Mrs. Morris (with whom he was living at the time) "is not that kind of an intellectual woman . . . I don't think I will encourage her writing. She would be far better occupied loving" (August 1923). Perhaps his most flagrantly sexist essay is the otherwise forgettable "Secret Drinking" (1932), in which he celebrates the Irish male camaraderie of drinking: "In other countries people drink out in the open air, in full view of passing traffic, with their wives, daughters, sisters; just as if they were having a cup of tea. An Irishman has a natural antipathy for drinking in public and as for drinking with women. . . . It's not done. We gave women the vote without any question but I curse the day when we give them the right to drink with us. It will ruin the country, kill all romance and put us on the same low level as the other countries" (110). Again, O'Flaherty reveals himself here as a reactionary in terms of gender roles.

The women with whom O'Flaherty lived during the 1920s were each, to some extent, his patrons. Margaret Barrington, who married him and bore his only child, Pegeen, offered him an entrée into upper-crust Dublin society because she was married to the well-known Trinity College historian Edmund Curtis when O'Flaherty met her. During their years together she was a careful editor of O'Flaherty's work. Earlier, in 1923, his letters to Garnett changed from typescript to longhand just after he left "Miss Casey"—because the typewriter was hers. He did feel remorseful about leaving her: "I couldn't do it. It's awful. Terrible torture to injure a *friend*. She has been a friend to me—the most sacred thing in life, a friend, a comrade. And to make her unhappy. This is awful" (19 June 1923). A few years earlier he had stayed with his sisters in Boston, "but as I am incapable of showing my feeling towards those whom I love intimately," he noted in *Two Years*, "they thought me cold" (296). In April 1924 he sent Garnett "a story by a friend of mine, a young woman, which I think is very good, because it's very true to life. She knows these damn people better than I do because I suppose she is a woman." In the same month he wrote that "women are very queer and"—he admitted in his most confessional comment on the subject—"I do not understand them very well."

O'Flaherty had grown up observing women who were closely confined within the rigid gender roles found in traditional rural Irish societies such as Inis Mór. Several of his stories depict these gender roles. Even well-known stories describing apparently idyllic young mating and marriage relationships, such as "Spring Sowing" and "Milking Time," contain within them suggestions of the darker side of gender differentiation from the point of view of Aran women. "Spring Sowing" (1924), the title story of O'Flaherty's first volume of stories, is an elegiac delineation of a young couple's pride and pleasure in "the first day of their first spring sowing as man and wife" (*Cormorant*, 1). Martin and Mary Delaney exchange terms of endearment translated from the Irish, such as "'pulse of my heart, treasure of my life,' and such traditional phrases" (2). They experience their relationship, however, in different ways. Martin "looked at his wife's little round black head and felt very proud of having her as his own" (5). As Angeline Kelly points out, in the field he "'absolutely without thought' works furiously for he, as a male, is already proving himself," whereas Mary "walks with 'furrowed' brows seized by a sudden terror as she realises the extent of her double enslavement, to the earth, and to her body" (12–13). For Mary "a momentary flash of rebellion against the slavery of being a peasant's wife crossed her mind. It passed in a moment" (7). The young couple's positive feelings at the end of the story are undercut by a grimmer prognosis: "They had done it together. They had planted seeds in the earth. The next day and the next and all their lives, when spring came they would have to bend their backs and do it until their hands and bones got twisted with rheumatism. But night would always bring sleep and forgetfulness" (8).

Similarly, at the end of "Milking Time" (1925) Michael and Kitty walk home romantically, "silently hand in hand, in the twilight" (*Cormorant*, 80), but they too are characterized in sentences notable for the mix of present satisfaction with darker premonitions as well as for a syntactic complexity that runs counter to O'Flaherty's celebrated simple style: "It was like a ceremony, this first milking together, initiating them into the mysterious glamour of mating; and both their minds were awed at the new strange knowledge that had come to their simple natures, something that belonged to them both, making their souls conscious of their present happiness with a dim realization of the great struggle that would follow it, struggling with the earth and the sea for food. And this dim realization tinged their happiness with a gentle sadness, without which happiness is ever coarse and vulgar" (79).

Stories such as "Selling Pigs" (1924) and "The Reaping Race" (1924) show that the longer Aran couples endure, the more their lives are subsumed by economic and traditional forces. Michael and Mary Derrane have been married for only six months, but already the art of negotiating the sale of their pigs is central to their experience. "The Reaping Race" is a version of Aesop's "The Tortoise and the Hare" in which communal ritual is dominant. All of the participants, for example, wear traditional garb. Out to prove that slow and steady will indeed win the race, the eventual victors are a married couple thoroughly ensconced in well-practiced roles:

> Nobody took any notice of Gill and his wife, but they had never stopped to eat and they had steadily drawn nearer to their opponents. . . . Then, when they reached the stone at half-way, Gill quietly laid down his hook and told his wife to bring the meal. She brought it from the fence, buttered oaten bread and a bottle of new milk with oatmeal in the bottom of the bottle. They ate slowly and then rested for a while. People began to jeer at them when they saw them resting, but they took no notice. After about twenty minutes they got up to go to work again.
> (*Short Stories*, 205)

In disgust over her husband's exhaustion, Kate Considine takes over from him—"I'll carry on myself" (206)—but it is too late to stop the Gills from winning.

Life is hard for everyone on the Aran Islands, but generally O'Flaherty shows that it is a man's world if it is anyone's. Gender roles are particularly separate and stereotyped in his stories of childhood and youth. He tends to show young boys as taking pleasure and pride in receiving affection and gifts from their parents and in moving toward manhood, in stories such as "Fishing" (1924), "Swimming" (1924),

"Mother and Son" (1925), "The Test of Courage" (1943), and "The New Suit" (1943) or "An Chulaith Nua" (1946). In "Fishing," for example, a father saves himself and his son from the rough tide and declares, "You darling, you were worth getting drowned for. So you were."[61]

The maternal bond is similarly strong in "Mother and Son," which appears clearly drawn from O'Flaherty's own relationship with his storytelling mother. After coming home late, the son narrates to his mother a fabulous vision of a horse running through the air, and thus gains forgiveness: "'Sure you won't tell on me, mother?' '"No, treasure, I won't.' '"On your soul you won't?' '"Hush! little one. Listen to the birds. They are beginning to sing. I won't tell at all. Listen to the beautiful ones.' "They both sat in silence, listening and dreaming, both of them" (*Short Stories*, 186).

O'Flaherty almost entirely neglects girlhood in his stories. When he does focus on female adolescence in "An Scáthán" or "The Mirror" (1953), in which he describes a girl taking pleasure in seeing herself naked for the first time, O'Flaherty can only imagine, as Kelly notes, "the male reaction" and place it "in the mind of the girl who is physically affected by the sight exactly as most men would be" (20). This story ends by assigning her to the status of "a radiant virgin wantoning naked in the sunlight on silken moss and no longer afraid in the least of love's awe-inspiring fruit, the labour of pregnancy" (*Cormorant*, 233).

Passion is everything in O'Flaherty's vision of positive bonds between the sexes, as in his view of many aspects of life. His stories repeatedly suggest that woman and man together are best occupied making love and producing children. His essential model is drawn from Aran animal life as captured in "The Water Hen" (1938) or "An Chearc Uisce" (1953), in which the cock knows no sexual repression; after defeating his opponent in a fight over a water hen, "in a moment he was upon her and she lay down in a swoon" (*Cormorant*, 157). A human version of this story is "The Caress" (1934), which O'Flaherty positioned at the end of *Shame the Devil* to demonstrate that writing it had allowed him to overcome writer's block—thus directly linking artistic creativity to sexual passion. In this story Martin Derrane and Mary Madigan make love wantonly in the grass and then prepare to escape to America, leaving behind old drunken Delaney and his would-be arranged match with Mary.

A more powerful and realistic story, however, is "Teangabháil" or "The Touch" (1946), with a plot directly opposed to that of "The Caress." Here Kate Hernon's desire for Brian O'Neill, whom she is able to embrace only briefly, is crushed by her father, who has arranged her marriage to an older neighboring farmer and utterly rejects Brian, a mere laborer on the Hernon farm: "First she thought of her hands touching his hands and of his bosom touching her breasts and of the intoxication produced in her by that touch. Then the sorrow of eternal hell followed close upon that drunkening thought, as she realised that this first touch of love would be the last touch and that she was henceforth sold to a man whose touch would be a torture to her flesh," (*Cormorant*, 150). A few other stories portraying victimized women and evil men—"The Tyrant" (1926), "The Ditch" (1929), and "The Outcast" (1925)—similarly picture young women as victims of a patriarchal, marriage-market, priest-ridden island culture. "The Tyrant" (1926) tells the story of a woman who finally leaves her hateful attorney husband. "The Ditch" (1929) describes the victimization of a poor woman by an ignorant and fearful young farm laborer who kills her newborn baby that he fathered. "The Outcast" (1925) was assessed and summarized by O'Flaherty to Garnett as "another short story of which I am proud . . . a servant girl, cast out of a village by the parish priest, because she has a child, drowns herself in a mountain lake" (22 October 1924).

Some other stories fix themselves on men who make fools of themselves because of their misdirected passion. Though not among O'Flaherty's better stories, they are worth mentioning because they further complicate his varied treatment of gender. The protagonist of "The Fall of Joseph Timmins" (1929) tries to force himself on his maid, only to be immediately witnessed by his nephew, to whom he has to agree therefore to give the money for which the nephew has been asking. In several stories men are duped by women. "The Intellectual" (1925) concerns a schoolmaster infatuated with a young woman who flirts with him and then laughs at him behind his back with her boyfriend. Very similarly, in "The Sensualist" (1926) a hotel proprietress at whom a visiting attorney makes a pass tells him to wait for her in his room, and then goes to bed with the hotel manager instead, with both of them mocking the attorney. In "Unclean" (1932) a man visits a prostitute in Dublin, but she tricks him out of his money and he becomes the laughingstock of the slum. It is significant that each of these foolish men is a middle-class or upper-class person—an unusual type of protagonist in O'Flaherty's stories. In these cases sexism is closely tied to class conflict in a manner distinct from most of the aforementioned Aran stories, except for "The Touch," in which the farm laborer is spurned by the farm owner.

At the same time, O'Flaherty was capable of the most offensive chauvinism, not only in his letters and essays but also in a few of his otherwise most forgettable stories. In "The Sinner" (1929) he informs us that Julia Rogers, when possessed by her brutish husband, Buster, "shuddered in ecstasy at the realization of all the happiness which life is capable of giving a woman."[62] This from the author of "The Touch"! Stories like this were not included in O'Flaherty's best-known collections—I strongly suspect that he wrote them for the money. As he remarked in *Two Years*, "Even now when I am weaving tales, I am unhappy because I have to sell them in order to buy leisure for weaving more. I have sometimes to think of the future" (14). The clearest example of this failing is "Indian Summer," a story that no one would ever guess was written by O'Flaherty if the proof of his authorship did not exist. Published in *Good Housekeeping*, and obviously aimed at the American housewife and motivated by profit, this lamentable story describes two Americans who fall in love while on vacation in Cuba, complete with a flowery happy ending and accompanied (thanks to the editors) by a sappy romantic picture of the business-executive hero reclining in his bathrobe. Following O'Flaherty's byline there is no indication within the story itself, which was never anthologized, that it was written by an Irish writer. Similarly, "Light" (1948) portrays lovemaking on a Caribbean beach, and "The Mermaid" (1929) was an unfortunate romance penned for *John O'London's Weekly*.

O'Flaherty's occasionally maudlin, sexist presentation of gender in his stories cannot be dismissed entirely as a sell-out to the periodical marketplace. One of his more frequently anthologized and longest stories, "The Wedding" (1946), conveys the message that women are happy only if they are married. Here a 43-year-old woman's wedding creates sharp jealousy in her unmarried neighbor. Likewise, "The Lament" (1941) centers on the desperate emotions of an unmarried woman who is attracted to a young man from Dublin who hires her father's boat near Galway to go to Inis Mór. Although only 26, "she had a horrid feeling that this was the turning-point in her life, that she had missed her last chance of happiness and that the future was going to be barren."[63]

O'Flaherty also falls prey to the virgin-or-whore syndrome. The protagonist of "Josephine" (1924) cannot have the young man to whom she is attracted, so she agrees to marry a man on the mainland whom she does not love simply to escape Inis Mór, meanwhile planning to indulge her sexual desires in extramarital encounters. This was one of the stories that he felt would prevent good sales in Ireland of the volume in which it appeared, *Spring Sowing*, as noted to Garnett (16 May 1924). The story ends as follows: "After all, Ballymullan was on the mainland within easy reach of Dublin. There would be social calls, week-end trips and a liberal allowance. . . . Anything was better than Inverara in winter. And perhaps the curate in Ballymullan. . . . And Josephine smiled again."[64] In *Two Years* O'Flaherty recorded the opinion that "the harlot is a poacher on the rights of marriage, which, in turn, is the respectable woman's chief means of livelihood. The harlot, to put it crudely, retails what the respectable woman sells wholesale for a fixed annuity, and various other emoluments, personal and social" (12). In this view a woman is either a virgin, unfulfilled because excluded from sex and procreation, or a whore, bartering sex for security whether within marriage or on the streets.

Complicating such sharp sexism, however, are the stories already considered in which women are presented as sympathetic victims of evil men and traditional patriarchy, and also other stories whose protagonists are strong older women whom O'Flaherty clearly admired. He indicated to Garnett that "Red Barbara" (1928) was "a great story. . . . Yes, it's a good one—about the beautiful widow of Feeney the fisherman. She refused to conceive of a weaver" (1 July 1927). On one level, the story is a "fable" (self-described in the last sentence of the story) of pagan passion opposed to Christian repression. In contrast to "The Fairy Goose," however, in which the priest makes sure that paganism is brutally obliterated, here erotic paganism wins out over Christianity when Barbara rejects Joseph (whose name echoes the biblical Mary's celibate husband) and remarries after his death, choosing "a dark young fisherman, who had wrists like steel" (*Cormorant*, 139), and bears him children. On another level, "Red Barbara" is a grim realistic tale that shows that Barbara is not at all entirely either the mythical heroine or the modern liberated woman we might otherwise expect or hope from this dénouement. Her first husband before Joseph "had treated her sometimes with cruelty, but she understood him and was happy as his wife. When he threw her down with violence and embraced her she was content. At other times he fondled her like a child.

Often he was drunk and beat her. She used to wait patiently for him in the town, standing in the road outside a tavern, while he got drunk with the neighbours. That was not pleasant, but it was the custom among the people" (133). Unhappy with and mystified by the ascetic Joseph, Barbara strongly reaffirms this peasant life-style by marrying the fisherman at the end. "She was a happy woman of the people once more. . . . She led him staggering from the town, singing drunkenly, to her wild bed" (139).

The later story "The Old Woman" (1948) shows a rare willingness to examine women apart from sex, procreation, or men. Like "The Wedding" (1946), which was written during the same period, "The Old Woman" is unusual in its focus on women interacting among themselves in the absence of men, and it is even more atypical because its characters are not obsessed with marriage and in fact do not talk about men at all. Old Maggie Crampton visits Julia Duggan and her daughter. "Her lips moved in prayer. Strands of white hair hung down on either side of her wrinkled yellow cheeks. The colour had almost completely faded from the pupils of her eyes. She had no teeth left" (*Cormorant*, 213). But by the end of the story Maggie emerges as a courageous voice countering Julia's skepticism and negativity about the ugly things in life: "'There are only lovely things in God's world,' she kept muttering as she advanced slowly up the lane with her hands on her knees. "The little white bag swung gently to and fro with each step" (221). "The Old Woman" appears to represent a departure in O'Flaherty's treatment of women as well as Christianity. Written during his last period of publication, the story prompts wonder about whether he might have gone on to write more stories in this vein if indeed he had chosen to continue publishing after the early 1950s.

O'Flaherty's most ambitious treatment of the relation of male and female was his long tale *The Ecstasy of Angus*, published in 1931 in a 58-page edition limited to 365 signed copies. It is singular in its length—intermediate between his generally truly short stories and his full-length novels (though much closer in length to some of his longer stories such as "The Wedding"). Even more so, it is unique as the only fabulist, nonrealist work of fiction he ever published. Unlike even "The Fairy Goose" and "Red Barbara," which incorporate folkloric and mythical elements within realist narratives, *The Ecstasy of Angus* is a philosophical tale set amidst the ancient Irish mythical world of Angus and Fand. O'Flaherty appears to have remained attached to this work. He chose, 47 years after its initial publication, to fill two-and-a-half sides of his 1978 double-album recording (including also "Red Barbara" and "Dúil") with his rendition of it, in the same year in which it was reprinted by Wolfhound Press. The gist of the story, following a well-known mythical motif, is that Angus enjoys sex with Fand and produces a son ("Genius," the first man in this creation myth), but at the expense of his youth, beauty, property, and life. Fand successfully tempts Angus not with an apple, but with her body: " 'Here between the snowy mounds of my breasts, soft, swooning love shall overcome the memory of that foolish vow, which the jealous ignorance of your father Youth imposed on you, lest Angus, grown to Manhood through the food of wisdom, should reach a magnificence beyond the comprehension of the gods themselves. Sleep, sweet love, while I bear you to my magic tent. There you shall awaken to find my promises do not do justice to the ecstasy you shall experience.' "[65] Assisted by erotic fairies, the aggressive Fand enacts her seduction of and copulation with Angus according to her own dictates. For Angus only "submission changed the pain of laceration into ecstasy" (33). As Kelly emphasized in her 1978 afterward, Fand "emerges as dominant, not subject to or emanating from the male as Eve did. Male and female are thus polarized. Male/female mutual dependency follows, with potential for both cooperation and antagonism" (61).

Further, "Genius" is "born victim of an inescapable duality," Kelly notes, "for which he himself is not responsible" (60). This is the tension between *agape* and *eros*, between love and lust. It is interesting and significant that O'Flaherty presents this conflict between love and lust, rather than love and pride, as the source of his original sin (or most basic flaw). Writing presumably just as he was about to separate from his wife (which he stated in his final letter to Garnett, of 3 March 1932, that he had already done), he tacitly recognizes lust as the defining male imperfection. He celebrated passion above all else, but his aforementioned stories about foolish males misled by lust, as well as *The Ecstasy of Angus*, demonstrate that passion can involve lust as well as love and can be destructive as well as constructive. The birth of "Genius" from sin reflects his ambivalence.

This duality or conflict between love and lust, like the strain between the "servile" and "insolent" sides of O'Flaherty's peasant status, may help us to explain the apparent contradiction between the clear presence of misogyny in his writing and those stories that present women as victimized or strong and men as foolish or evil. Such tensions are in turn closely linked to perhaps the most basic cultural disparity

Naturalism

"Silence. It was noon. The sea was calm" (*Cormorant*, 95). Above on top of a cliff, a goat took fright and dislodged a stone, which fell and wounded one of the cormorants in the flock resting below in the sea. The flock turned on the disabled bird, rejecting it and eventually killing it:

> They had no mercy. They fell upon it fiercely, tearing at its body with their beaks, plucking out its black feathers and rooting it about with their feet. It struggled madly to creep in farther on the ledge, trying to get into a dark crevice in the cliff to hide, but they dragged it back again and pushed it towards the brink of the ledge. One bird prodded its right eye with its beak. Another gripped the broken leg firmly in its beak and tore at it.
>
> At last the wounded bird lay on its side and began to tremble, offering no resistance to their attacks. Then they cackled loudly, and, dragging it to the brink of the ledge, they hurled it down. . . .
>
> Then it fluttered its wings twice and lay still. An advancing wave dashed it against the side of the black rock and then it disappeared, sucked down among the seaweed strands.
>
> (98)

This is the gist of "The Wounded Cormorant" (1925), one of O'Flaherty's many closely observed and vividly described animal stories. Like a number of his other stories, this one depicts a harsh, Darwinian, naturalistic world in which only the fittest survive (and sometimes even they meet cruel fates). Stories of this kind are among O'Flaherty's most frequently anthologized works, and have been central in the forming of his reputation. As a result, "O'Flaherty has often been described," Ben Forkner notes, "as the most 'naturalistic' of the Irish realists."[67]

Like naturalistic pioneers such as Émile Zola and Jack London, O'Flaherty was well prepared to see human existence as animalistic and had excellent credentials to write about animals. He grew up on Inis Mór surrounded by animal life within a culture thoroughly dependent on fish, cows, and other animals to provide food and a livelihood.

He never lost his close concentration on animal life, often conjuring up the animals of the Aran Islands in his mind even when he lived in London, Dublin, or New York. Take this passage in *Shame the Devil,* for example: "Just now a weasel is more important to me than any woman. A weasel I saw last year in Aran looking over a stone wall that surrounds a sally garden. How beautiful its throat looked and the line of its supple body. It had its head upraised and it was smelling the air. It smelt me, got startled and then glided away so quickly that my staring eyes could still see it peering over the fence after it had gone" (75). Later, while at the racetrack, "by some freak of the imagination" he sees "a rabbit that had lost its way one morning in a cliff at home" (84). O'Flaherty repeatedly returns in his mind both to the stalking weasel and the hunted rabbit, and eventually identifies himself (when down on his luck) with the "rabbit squealing" (92). Later he describes his interaction with a sand insect in Donegal (204–5).

O'Flaherty's careful attention to animals is frequently made evident in his letters to Garnett. His references to animals in these private documents demonstrate that animal life for him was not merely a literary subject, but held a fascination in its own right, wherever he was. In April 1923, for example, he wrote from England, "I sat for two hours in a field yesterday watching young heifers. It's peculiar the way they lie down. Invariably they raise snouts in the air and blow out their breath. I think it's to clear their nostrils. . . . I never noticed this before." He noted that "The Blackbird" (1924) was written "about a blackbird I saw in Stephen's Green" in Dublin (April 1924). While living outside Enniskerry, County Wicklow, south of Dublin, in the spring of 1926, he described snipe, a bittern, pigeons, other birds, rabbits, and goats. He took particular notice of the birthing experiences of the goats, detailing the contrasting reactions of the different mother goats and finding one to be "a wonderful character but a hopeless milker. I shot her kids and in revenge she is deliberately withholding her milk, so that very probably she will go dry in a fortnight unless she changes her mind and decides to behave herself. I think she is a most unhappy animal for she wails at times for no reason in the world. Possibly she is infected with the Bolshevist idea" (15 May 1926).

Following a visit to Inis Mór, he reflected that "the people are sadly inferior to the island itself. But the sea birds are almost worthy of it. The great cormorants thrilled me. And while fishing . . . a great bull seal rose from the sea in front of me. He looked at me with brutal drunken eyes and then dived. Father says they have nests there in caves" (17 June 1927). On another occasion he cited an old Irish proverb that is interesting not only because it involves an animal but also because O'Flaherty recalled it while ruminating about his divided life (torn between Aran and the big cities and driven by personal and cultural conflicts): "The sandlark cannot have both beaches at the one time" (July 1925).

In his classic study of literary naturalism, Charles Walcutt identified the deterministic paradigms of Darwin and Marx as important influences and stressed, "The major themes and motifs are *determinism, survival, violence,* and *taboo.*"[68] These are also central themes in the stories of O'Flaherty, who knew very well from growing up on Aran the truth of Hemingway's maxim that "all stories, if continued far enough, end in death."[69] In *Shame the Devil,* he expressed the eminently naturalistic opinion that "life is an interminable process of one form of life preying on another, from the cow that destroys life in the blade of grass, to the lion that leaps upon a stag in the African forest" (55). He added that "when a man is born on naked rocks like the Aran Islands, where the struggle for life against savage nature is very intense, the instinct for self-preservation is strong in him" (10).

Throughout O'Flaherty's short fiction there runs a strong naturalistic streak—the most critically celebrated aspect of his work. At the same time, it is equally clear that O'Flaherty was no simple naturalistic writer, and that a number of his stories affirm passion and life rather than portray determinism and death. Forkner aptly recognizes that "his brand of naturalism has very little in common with the self-satisfied certitudes of Continental writers. Always there prevails a deep sense of mystery in the face of uncontrollable passions" (670). Given his naturalistic streak and his preoccupation with animals, one might expect O'Flaherty to look to Zola; Paul Doyle reports that his sister Delia Ó hEithir and her husband Pádraic indicated that O'Flaherty admired Zola (120), but as I suggested earlier (see note 25), the Ó hEithirs were sometimes unreliable. In fact, though in his letters to Garnett O'Flaherty praises Turgenev, Chekhov, Gorki, Dostoyevski, Conrad, Lawrence, and Joyce, he never mentions Zola.

O'Flaherty's innate rebelliousness and belief in passion meant that his naturalistic convictions could be no more doctrinaire than his Marxism. He made clear his response to determinism in *I Went to Russia;* confronted by a Marxist version of determinism in practice, "I felt like saying, 'I'd rather disembowel myself like a Jap than be a cog in your machine'" (37). As James O'Brien writes concerning his novels, "although O'Flaherty has naturalistic leanings, he never makes the meticulous examination of environment of a Zola or Dreiser, in part because in his work environment does not control the protagonist. Instead, O'Flaherty's chief characters, often driven by obsessions, plunge into disaster" (36). Angeline Kelly adds that "for O'Flaherty the real horror is not violence, which is always an expression of passion, however thwarted or misdirected this may be, but a satiated indifference or apathy which does not exist in nature" (84).

Even when focusing (as he so often does) on animals, who are controlled by their environment more obviously than people are, O'Flaherty's view of nature is not monolithic, but multifarious. Positioned right before "The Wounded Cormorant," that most grimly naturalistic story, in the 1973 collection to which the story lent its title, is "The Wild Goat's Kid" (1925), in which a mother goat successfully wards off and kills a dog who attacks her kid; immediately after "Cormorant" is "Birth" (1926), in which a cow has a healthy calf that it licks "savagely" with "great love" (*Cormorant*, 104), in an ending also clearly meant to counterbalance "The Cow's Death." O'Flaherty mentioned to Garnett that he and his wife "claim that it's as good as 'The Cow's Death,'" although "perhaps it lacks the power of tragedy" (21 July 1926). A similar story is "Three Lambs" (1924), in which a young boy witnesses and delights in the nearly miraculous birth of three female lambs in a single litter.

Nature giveth and nature taketh away. Considered as a whole, O'Flaherty's short stories balance life and death in nature, variously describing people, animals, and inanimate natural forces. Many of his stories are accurately enough assessed as naturalistic; others must be called counternaturalistic or even antinaturalistic. Indeed, some of his stories must be removed from this context altogether, to be interpreted, as other sections of this book clearly demonstrate. Doyle correctly stresses that "O'Flaherty combines Naturalistic and Romantic qualities" (121). Perhaps most apt of all is Seán Ó Faoláin's description of O'Flaherty as an "inverted Romantic."[70] Following naturalism, O'Flaherty emphasized the entrapped, tragic fate of both animals and people, but solace and beauty were always to be found in primitive, passionate Nature, the romantically unifying principle beyond innocence and despair.

O'Flaherty's nature stories reflect his rural, primitive settings and active, "simple," visual style. Kelly notes that "an analysis of O'Flaherty's stories shows that three-fifths of them are set in the open air" (128), and Helene O'Connor adds that they "should find an appreciative new audience of contemporary readers who have recently begun to recognize the importance of ecology."[71] Deborah Averill claims that "O'Flaherty's preference for wild and rugged terrain recalls Daniel Corkery more than any other previous story writer. . . . But Corkery associates natural objects with religious and moral values . . . whereas O'Flaherty regards nature simply as a blind, indifferent force which man may temporarily conquer, but which will eventually destroy him."[72] It was in O'Flaherty's naturalistic stories about animals and people, more than anywhere else, that he fashioned his famously blunt, active, visual style. In this respect "The Cow's Death" appears to have been his big breakthrough; he proudly emphasized to Garnett that this story had "that feeling of coldness" for which he was striving (5 May 1923). Certainly the story succeeds: "For a long time the cow stood leaning over the fence, until the pain lessened. She turned around suddenly and lowed and tossed her head. She took a short run forward, the muscles of her legs creaking like new boots. She stopped again, seeing nothing about her in the field. Then she began to run around by the fence, putting her head over it here and there, lowing. She found nothing. Nothing answered her call" (*Cormorant*, 10). Kelly argues that "by expressing satisfaction with the effect he achieved in 'The Cow's Death' O'Flaherty has given us a yardstick by which we can measure the degree of detachment or 'coldness' he achieved, or failed to achieve, in his other short stories" (53). His insistence to Garnett at another point that he wanted to have "no style" (3 April 1924) appears to have been a rejection of the stereotypically flowery prose style of many nineteenth-century fiction writers. O'Flaherty set himself the task of creating a style facilitating the illusion that his stories simply provided an objective, visual "lens" on the actual experiences of animals and people—a style that would appear to be "no style." As Kelly puts it, "in O'Flaherty's better stories one feels, indeed, that the story has written itself" (128).

These stories are strongly visual and direct, reminding one of films. Like Joyce, O'Flaherty was very interested in film. He relished the success of John Ford's version of *The Informer*, and noted in *I Went to Russia*, "I love this new art of the cinematograph" (224). As Kelly points out, "Professor Delargy has said that 'the film is the modern folktale.' Both A. E. Coppard and Elizabeth Bowen compared the short

story to the film, for visual images now take first place over the speaking voice" (39).

Perhaps O'Flaherty's visual naturalism is purest in stories describing
natural forces, such as "The Wave" (1924), "The Flood" (1925), "The
Tide" (1948), and "An Charraig Dhubh" (1953). Each of these stories
concentrates on the effect of rising and falling tidewaters, which is not
surprising in view of the fact that, as O'Flaherty stressed in *Two Years*,
"I have the sea in my blood. . . . I was born in a fishing village, within
earshot of the great Atlantic main that licks the cliff-bound shores of
Aran" (75). In comparable fashion to (but more vividly sensual than)
Yeats's hankering after "The Lake Isle of Innisfree" while walking
through the streets of London, in *Shame the Devil* O'Flaherty recounted
his intense longing for Aran while pacing his room in New York: "Oh,
God! Could I only hear the rumble of sweet water leaping through its
tunnel beneath a falling field and see its emergence from the dark
brown clay in a little nook, round which in bygone days the people of
my village had built a wall of stones, now covered with lichen? Could
I only put my face beneath its silver spout and feel its soothing freshness on my eyelids?" (153–54). At the end of *Two Years* he celebrated
his return to the island: "A godless hermit, I began my communion
with the cliffs, the birds, the wild animals, and the sea of my native
land" (351).

"The Wave" and "An Charraig Dhubh" (The black rock) are very
similar: each vividly describes the powerfully destructive impact of the
sea, which in "The Wave" crushes a 200-foot-high cliff with which it
had been fighting for centuries, and similarly destroys a large bolder at
its edge in "An Charraig Dhubh." The latter story, one of those that
was never published in English, is remarkable for its photographically
specific analyses of the adaptations to the rising and falling tide by
several forms of plant and animal life living on or near the rock, before
its destruction by the sea—including "míola mara" (sea creatures),
"bair nigh" (limpets), "dúilicíní" (mussels, their eyes opening and
closing rhythmically like accordians), "caonach" (sea moss, a form of
plant life nearly as active as the mussels), "frídí" (mites), "faochain"
(periwinkles), "éiscíni" (little fish), "portáin" (crabs), "péiste móire"
(a monster whale), "faoileán" (a seagull), and "conablach ronnaigh" (a
mackerel carcass). Such specific visual detail is like something out of a
National Geographic article or a Jacques Cousteau film. The sea is described as "ag bualadh agus ag bualadh gan sos, leis na mílte agus na

mílte bliain" (*Dúil,* 25, beating and beating without rest, for thousands and thousands of years), until it shatters the rock altogether.

"The Flood" similarly describes the adjustments of insect life to the rising and falling of a river—though O'Flaherty dismissed this story to Garnett (who had criticized it) as "an example of what can come out of O'Flaherty's brain when he is getting a neurasthenic fit" (19 November 1924). "The Tide" is the most objective and detached story in this group; set somewhere in subtropical America and probably written sometime in the early 1940s during his years in the United States, it simply narrates in straightforward fashion the comings and goings of people, animals, and the tide at a beach between early morning and sunset. If O'Flaherty had combined the even more graphic portrait of natural life on Aran found in "An Charraig Dhubh" with the more detached point of view (free of gratuitous, cataclysmic destruction by the sea) in "The Tide," he would have achieved a story greater than any of these fascinating but somewhat flawed sketches.

Frank O'Connor said of O'Flaherty that "his subject is instinct, not judgement," and Æ felt that "when O'Flaherty thinks, he's a goose; when he feels, he's a genius." [73] As Patrick Sheeran points out, O'Flaherty's devotion to "stories of wild animals and birds is not surprising in view of the frequency with which animal tales occur in the folklore of the region" (48) and the fact that "the seaboard of Galway had more unrecorded folktales in 1935 . . . than had all the rest of Western Europe" (46). Garnett may have encouraged O'Flaherty to write about the animals of Aran, but nobody was already so well qualified to do so as he. Of his naturalistic stories centering on the inevitable fate of animals, I have already highlighted "The Cow's Death" and "The Wounded Cormorant," the most unforgettable ones. Also notable in this category are such stories as "Two Dogs" (1923), "The Foolish Butterfly" (1924), "Prey" (1927), "The Black Rabbit" (1929), "The Blackbird's Mate" (1929), "All Things Come of Age" (1935), "An Fiach" (1953), and "Wild Stallions" (1976). The earliest and latest of these portray pairs of animals of the same species in competition or combat. In "Two Dogs" a veteran mongrel, intensely jealous of a greyhound recently brought into the house by his master, is gratified when the greyhound plunges to his death over a cliff while chasing a rabbit. Similarly, a golden stallion kills a grey invading rival in "Wild Stallions," but is crippled in the process and killed himself by mountain lions. In this late story, which Brendan Kennelly feels could be read and scanned like verse, O'Flaherty wandered far from Aran to a setting somewhere presumably in the American West. In several other stories animals prey upon other animals in Darwinian fashion. A rabbit is the most common victim—killed by cats in "The Black Rabbit," by a dog in "An Fiach" (The hunt), and by a weasel in "All Things Come of Age" (an uncharacteristically moralizing rather than objective title referring to the baby rabbit for whom its mother has sacrificed itself, who must now commence life on its own). In "Prey"—"of which I am proud" (11 June 1927), O'Flaherty noted to Garnett—birds alight upon an apparently dead ass and are subsequently driven away by dogs. Nearly as often, however, animals are victimized not by others but by their own innocent natures. "The Foolish Butterfly" flies out over the sea and inevitably drowns. "The Blackbird's Mate" freezes to death in the dead of winter after refusing to leave her eggs.

"The Hawk" and its mate fall prey to other kinds of animals: men. In this excellent story, which O'Flaherty read on Radio Éireann in 1957 (Kelly, 128), he carefully parallels the two species. First the male hawk kills a lark, "his brute soul . . . exalted by the consciousness that he had achieved the fullness of the purpose for which nature had endowed him" (*Cormorant*, 224–25). But then he must watch men snatch his mate and put her in a bag, feeling "helpless in the presence of the one enemy that he feared by instinct" (225) and dying in his futile attempt to ward them off. These men emerge as merely other animals, only more dangerous. O'Flaherty's earlier story "The Wren's Nest" (1924), in which a boy destroys a nest, suggests that such harsh practice is learned early. Like several other stories that link animals and people in this way, "The Hawk" suggests that birds and men are simply creatures within the same naturalistic universe. Not only are people often presented as animalistic; animals are given personal emotions and, as Kelly notes, are "called 'he' or 'she'" in all of O'Flaherty's stories "except 'The Foolish Butterfly' and 'The Wounded Cormorant' which both represent their species, and remain sexless" (10). Kelly makes the distinction that O'Flaherty's animals "are either in their wild state, dissociated from man, as in 'The Blackbird'; struggling against man as predator, as in 'The Rockfish'; or associated with man in his everyday life as in 'The Cow's Death'" (4)—adding that "when the peasant makes the sign of the cross on the cow's side" in the latter story, "man and cow are placed symbolically at one" (3). John Zneimer's point of view is that O'Flaherty "is not interested in how the animals are like people or how the people are like animals, but how both are manifestations of life and nature" (163). Zneimer argues that his stories strive to be not "about" nature but rather to *embody* nature in a coldly objective way.

In addition to the superior story "The Hawk," O'Flaherty's grimmest naturalistic stories linking animals and people include "The Black Mare" (1923), "The Black Bullock" (1924), "The Wild Sow" (1924), "The Salted Goat" (1924), and "Tidy Tim's Donkey" (1924). Written around the same time, each story reports the destruction of an animal by a foolish man—suggesting that from the beginning of his career as a writer, O'Flaherty was particularly struck by this aspect of life on Aran. Blaming folkloric fate rather than himself, the first-person narrator of "The Black Mare" nonetheless makes clear his own foolishness in racing his horse to its death when it falls onto large rocks. The folly of other protagonists is even more pronounced: Tidy Tim lets his donkey freeze to death, Old Neddy in "The Wild Sow" starves his pig until it breaks into his potato plot and chokes to death on one of his potatoes, and Patsy Halloran skins and salts his dead goat and is then found dead of starvation himself ("'The Salted Goat' gave me much satisfaction," O'Flaherty assured Garnett [13 September 1923]). "The Black Bullock," which to O'Flaherty seemed "to be all right" (22 November 1923), recounts the cruelest series of acts to an animal found anywhere in his fiction: a bullock that eats too much is rejected by its owner, tortured by people and other animals alike, and eventually falls, breaks its spine, and is slaughtered. Stories such as these implicitly criticize human exploitation of animals, emphasizing their domination in ways that counter the strong positive link between people and animals in some of the other stories. O'Flaherty's twice-repeated description of his chief heroic animal, the cow in "The Cow's Death," as "stupid" (*Cormorant*, 10) is one of several indications that to some extent he was capable of sharing as well as criticizing the Aran islanders' attitude toward animals.

Nor are people exempt from cruel fates within the naturalistic world of Aran. In "The Oar" (1928) a "mighty wave" arrives and destroys a crew of three fishermen, with O'Flaherty's folkloric use of threes injected into his naturalistic and gothic descriptions: "The third time the lightning flashed, they looked and saw nothing but a wall of sea approaching them" (*Cormorant*, 110). As for the survivors in another boat, "First they saw an upraised oar, raised straight on high, its handle grasped by an upraised face in agony. The face looked up, with staring eyes, as if saluting Heaven with his upraised oar. Then darkness came" (110). In the lesser story "The Struggle" (1924), two young men also drown at sea, but in this case it happens because of their drunken fight with each other. In another vein, O'Flaherty's great story "Going into Exile" (1924) shows that for parents, the departure of their children from Aran can seem as final as death. The grief of the mother, with her "dilated nostrils" and "bosom heaving," strongly recalls the reactions of the cow over its stillborn calf in "The Cow's Death," published a year earlier.

As forcefully as bleak naturalism runs through O'Flaherty's fiction, however, a romanticism insisting on the proud passions of both people and animals is just as strong, emerging as a romantic counterpoint to his naturalistic emphasis. Much as "Birth" appears to be a romantic, positive reply to "The Cow's Death," "The Landing" (1924) reads like the romantic companion piece to the naturalistic story "The Oar," with rough seas again terrifying people but the ending reversed in the victory of the fishermen over nature: "The boat and the crew and the men holding the boat were left on the rock, clinging to the rock and to one another, the way a dragged dog clings to the earth. They rushed up the rock with the boat. They had landed safely" (*Cormorant*, 35). Perhaps most clearly indicative of O'Flaherty's view of life and death and of romanticism and naturalism as inseparable conditions and attitudes are stories such as "The Stone" (1929) and "Life" (1947). It is notable that these stories appeared midway and late in O'Flaherty's writing career, while his darkest naturalistic stories appeared predominantly in the early 1920s. In "The Stone" an old man dies of a heart attack while trying to move a huge stone that he used to be able to lift. The end of the story, however, emphasizes not his defeat by nature, but rather the continuing human effort to live up to the challenge that he had earlier conquered: "And then, youths . . . challenged one another to a test of strength. They stripped themselves and began to tussle with the stone" (*Tavern*, 241). The cyclic nature of life and death is even clearer in "Life," which describes a grandfather's death and (immediately before it) his grandson's birth, with "the strong young heart . . . unaware that the tired old heart had just delivered up the life that made it beat" (*Cormorant*, 166).

Some other stories examined in previous chapters—such as "Desire," "The Caress," "Spring Sowing," and "Milking Time"—stress

the positive passions of people as overriding any premonitions of difficulty or death that they may have. Several stories depict animals as
proudly victorious over or at least surviving the forces of nature rather
than destroyed by them, by predators, or by themselves: "The Conger
Eel" (1924), "The Rockfish" (1924), "The Hook" (1924), "The
Blackbird" (1924), "A Crow Fight" (1924), "The White Bitch" (1924),
"The Lost Thrush" (1925), "The Little White Dog" (1927), "The
Water Hen" (1938), and "The Enchanted Water" (1952). O'Flaherty's
conger eel is perhaps his single most impressive animal. Caught for a
moment in the fishermen's net, he is pictured as an eight-foot-long
Irish Moby Dick who gets away and from whom the fishermen are glad
to escape: "Then stretching out to his full length he coursed in a wide
arc to his enormous lair, far away in the silent depths" (*Cormorant*, 85).
O'Flaherty's rockfish also gets away, in a story that Zneimer (157–60)
examines in detail. A more modest redaction of this motif of the animal
as triumphant over human foes is "The Hook," in which a seagull, with
the help of his mate, works his mouth free of a hook cruelly planted
by boys in a piece of liver. In "The Lost Thrush" a young bird, taken
home by a boy who becomes bored with it, is found by its parents.
Sentiment supplants forced naturalism in "The White Bitch": poor
people throw their pet dog into the sea because they lack the money
for a license, but then they retrieve her.[74] "The Blackbird" escapes
from a cat, and in "A Crow Fight" the mother crow loses her mate and
her nest, but successfully moves her babies to the nest of other crows
whose protestations she withstands. In "The Little White Dog," a
small terrier, fearful at first, stands up to and chases away a bull, then
becomes as bold and proud as if it were the great conger eel: "Now
and again he looked behind at the cheering boys. Then again he would
trot forward, with his foreleg bandied out and his tail raised aloft in a
curl" (*Tavern*, 214). Similarly, O'Flaherty's water birds are unvan-
quished in "The Water Hen" and "The Enchanted Water," with the
conquering cock mating with the object of his desire, and the untamed
drake eloping with one of a family's ducks and going to live on the
island's enchanted lake.

Thus, we find many stories countering the solemn naturalism so celebrated in O'Flaherty's short fiction, reminding us of his status as an
"inverted romantic" and of his central beliefs in passion and rebellion.
Reading the critics and O'Flaherty's most commonly anthologized and
therefore best-known stories, one might easily get the impression that

Satire and Comedy

In a hostile review in 1953 entitled "Liam O'Flaherty's Black and White World," John Crawford claimed that in *Dúil*, "blacks and whites are predominant," and that his is "a half-real world where violence and a kind of awkward sophistication are the only values." Admitting that "he writes fluently and gracefully in Irish that is a joy to read," Crawford felt that "Oifig an Phoist" ("The Post Office"), O'Flaherty's best-known comic story, was "pretty well a failure all round."[75] It was not so much O'Flaherty whose view was "black and white," but rather Crawford, who seemed unable to appreciate the complexity of O'Flaherty's work—perhaps because he had not read enough of it. An appreciation of the richness of O'Flaherty's work is reinforced by examining his use of satire and comedy.

"The Post Office" is in fact a very funny story, and it was just one of a number of such texts that are to be found, both early and later in O'Flaherty's career. Even the more intelligent and better informed scholars who appreciate "The Post Office" tend to assume that it was an isolated and belated "exception" in his career. Paul Doyle's comment is typical: "The most delightful story of O'Flaherty's later period, and a story most uncharacteristic of his career, is 'The Post Office.' Only on rare occasions does O'Flaherty evince a sense of humor throughout his writing career" (114). Brendan Kennelly similarly regrets "that O'Flaherty did not attempt more stories in the comic vein of 'The Post Office.'"[76]

"The Post Office" is indeed his best comic story, but to describe it as a rare example of comedy would be far from the truth. The best-known 1937 and 1956 anthologies served to encode mostly the naturalistic side of O'Flaherty's work, but Angeline Kelly's invaluable 1976 collection of 21 previously uncollected stories, *The Pedlar's Revenge*—as well as at least 30 more still-uncollected stories—include a number of other comic ones. Like his stories in general, a strong majority of these comic stories were first published in the 1920s, especially in the early 1920s. In *Liam O'Flaherty the Storyteller* Kelly points out that he "wrote thirty-eight short stories which are either humorous or contain some humor" (101). Kelly devotes a short chapter on "From Ridicule to Contempt" in the stories, which appears right between her chapters on violence and death and suggests in its title the tenor of her argument. In implicitly psychoanalytic fashion, she views O'Flaherty's humor as mostly a release mechanism and substitute for violence, and spends as much time on noncomic stories (such as "The Outcast") in order to argue this thesis. There is some truth to it in the case of the double-sided, complicated O'Flaherty. He probably belongs to the Irish comic tradition of the macabre and the grotesque as identified by Vivian Mercier, with these two types of humor helping us "to accept death and to belittle life," according to Mercier.[77] On the other hand, this point of view does not allow for the humanity and sheer fun of O'Flaherty's sense of humor at its most positive. Nor have other critics and scholars done justice to O'Flaherty's satire and comedy.[78]

In his seminal study *The Irish Comic Tradition*, Mercier identifies several other varieties of Irish humor expressed in Irish and in English writing from many different periods—including fantasy, wit and word play, satire, and parody. His argument for the continuity of Gaelic and "Anglo-Irish" comedy and satire makes particular sense in the case of a bilingual writer such as O'Flaherty. Interestingly, Mercier recognizes O'Flaherty as one of several twentieth-century Irish writers of satire (105), but he does nothing more than list his name. We ought to consider the full range of satire and comedy in O'Flaherty's short stories, linking them to his nonfictional comments on and uses of these kinds of writing. O'Flaherty's life and writings reflect the truth of two general comments about satirists and satire in general. One comes from Arthur Pollard's concise study, *Satire*: "The satirist is not an easy man to live with. He is more than usually conscious of the follies and vices of his fellows and he cannot stop himself from showing that he is."[79] The other is drawn from the earliest publication of Stephen Greenblatt: "The writing of satire . . . makes almost no demands for a particular belief or style."[80]

O'Flaherty's early realization that he wanted to experiment with comedy, not just write the naturalistic types of stories that Edward Garnett had encouraged, is recorded in several of his letters to Garnett. On 18 March 1924, he wrote: "In Ireland where nearly everybody takes himself seriously, it is very easy for a writer to see the silly side of himself. In England you all take yourselves seriously, all the time. That's what's the matter with England. The trouble with us in Ireland is that we have a sense of humour; now and again we see how ridiculous we are." A month later, he sent Garnett a story that he considered "very weak" but "a good lark" and worth including in a collection "if not on its merits as literature at least on its merits as a joke." At about the same time he mailed him a "flippant story," adding: "Whether I have succeeded in hiding its flippancy sufficiently under a cloak of art I don't know. I would rather like this method if it could be developed into anything worth while. But one is always looking for new methods and one is never satisfied" (11 April 1924). O'Flaherty complained when Garnett rejected "Colic" a few weeks later: "I think you should include it. In fact I must have it included as I consider it an excellent humourous story. You have a prejudice against humourous stories" (23 May 1924).

O'Flaherty's letters not only include such remarks about comedy, but often become bemused and amusing in their own right. For example, his letter of 16 July 1926 shows his comic imagination at work:

> How is your play going? I have already arranged in my own mind all the details of your first night, including your speech—which will include a tirade against the disturbance caused by Irish hooligans between the acts. These hooligans will be provided by me and also a band of respectable people to thrash them and throw them out. Then we might have a journalist hired—an honest fellow if we could get one—to rush down to his office with a description of the affair and there you are—headlines the next day—"Edward Garnett's Play Scene of Faction Fight—Great Speech by Garnett—Libel Action Threatened Against Author by Irish Free State" etc.

He wrote entertainingly about his newborn daughter in an undated letter: "The daughter is of course indifferent to her parents. Undoubtedly an O'Flaherty daughter therefore. Physically she is the image of her mother but I am afraid . . . born with my temper and ruthlessness. God help her suitors. Therefore, O benign Edward, stretch forth your spiritual hand to her . . . so that I may murmur in her tiny ears: 'You needn't scream. Edward Garnett is your godfather. Please don't disturb him.' This baby is so sensitive that when a man who I know is not a gentleman entered the room, she shuddered in her sleep." In his very last letter to Garnett, on 3 March 1932, O'Flaherty closed by indicating that "it's seven-thirty A.M. and I'm going to describe today the scoundrelly conduct of a certain Coleman O'Rourke. How awful life would be if the socialists exorcised rascality from the human gut."

Such "rascality" was the object of O'Flaherty's chief nonfictional satires: *The Life of Tim Healy, A Tourist's Guide to Ireland,* and *A Cure for Unemployment.* He offers an ironic critique of Healy's career. The narrator of *Tim Healy* is a classically satiric one, appearing to praise Healy where he would really have us condemn him. "The man who wrote" this book, he tells us in its preface, "must be as changeable as a weathercock in an uncertain wind" (6). This preface (excerpted in part 2) is in fact one of the funniest things O'Flaherty ever wrote. His *Tourist's Guide,* with a bitter tongue in cheek, satirically flays priest, politician, publican, and peasant. O'Flaherty is at his best on the priests: "Try to remember the name *Canon Sheehan.* There is no need to learn by rote the names of his books because the parish priest is likely to be ignorant of them himself. Apart from this reference to *Canon Sheehan,* literature must not be mentioned on any account. . . . Neither must education be discussed. The parish priest regards any references by a layman to education as a sign of Free Masonry [and] . . . any form of amusement as irreligious and dangerous to faith and morals" (31, 32). *A Cure for Unemployment* is O'Flaherty's most clearly Swiftian piece of writing, obviously influenced by "A Modest Proposal": "Do you know that there are six million, eight hundred and forty seven dogs in this country, of which one million, two hundred thousand, six hundred and eighty four are the property of citizens with an income of over a thousand a year. Roundly, my scheme is to substitute a human being as pet for every dog which is the property of a person with an income of over a thousand pounds a year. On the lowest estimate this would account for five hundred thousand fully grown unemployed men and women." Each of these works was published more than twenty years before "The Post Office." The preface to *Tim Healy* and many parts of the *Tourist's Guide* are in fact funnier than most of his stories.

When O'Flaherty turned to comedy in his short stories, his typical modes were farce and broad social comedy rather than satire. His avoidance of satire in his short fiction may have stemmed partly from his recognition of satire as a separate genre altogether, in the Swiftian manner. It may also be because he tried it but found that it did not work. In "The Adventures of General Michael Rathcrogan," a story–length manuscript in the O'Flaherty Collection at the Harry Ransom Humanities Research Center in Austin, Texas, he described in satiric fashion a character apparently known to both O'Flaherty and Garnett. A curiosity, this narrative is unfinished, unsuccessful, and unpublished. The closest thing to satire among O'Flaherty's published stories is "Benedicamus Domino" (1924), which exposes and ridicules the quirks and infidelities of various brothers in a monastery school (such as the one where O'Flaherty was a student). This is more of a realistic fictional exposé, however, than a true satire. An atypical story, it momentarily calls to mind Mervyn Wall's *The Unfortunate Fursey* (1946), but does not begin to approach the high quality of Wall's masterful satiric novel.

O'Flaherty wrote a number of farcical or low-comic stories, especially in the 1920s, including "A Shilling" (1924), "A Pot of Gold" (1924), "Patsa, or The Belly of Gold" (1928), "The Pedlar's Revenge" (1952), "Your Honour" (1925), "Colic" (1924), "The Stolen Ass" (1925), "The Bath" (1940), "The Jealous Hens" (1924), "The Bladder" (1924), "A Pig in a Bedroom" (1924), and "The Old Hunter" (1927). Significantly, only 4 of these 12 stories were among the more than 70 stories included in the best-known 1937 and 1956 anthologies of O'Flaherty's short fiction; as a result they are generally not mentioned in criticism on his work. Certainly the fact that most of them appeared in the 1920s contradicts the notion that comedy came only late to O'Flaherty. These stories tend to play out the comic "flip side" of the attempts of people and animals to survive (the same theme dominating his darkest naturalistic stories).

The human farces take people's ridiculous, competitive, deceptive grubbing for money as their most common subject. In "A Shilling," for example, several old men notice a coin fall from a man's pocket; the question is then which one of them can retrieve it without directly appearing to steal it. In "A Pot of Gold" O'Flaherty reenacted Pádraic Ó Conaire's trick on O'Flaherty himself, as mentioned in my chapter on his bilingualism: a man sends his friends to dig up a nonexistent pot of gold. In "Patsa, or The Belly of Gold" an Irish Midas figure swallows his gold in order to take it to the grave with him, but his wife forces it out of him with castor oil. A first-person narrator speaking as the voice of the community and similar to many of Frank O'Connor's narrators describes Patsa as an infamous character also known to accost visitors to Aran at the pier and bamboozle them through various ruses. O'Flaherty enjoys Patsa and implicitly derides Synge and other such visitors to his island, indicating that Patsa "told poets and scholars and dramatists, who are now famous, most of the legends and mystic lore that became current in Ireland and even in Europe during the past generation, relating to the Celtic Twilight" (*Pedlar's Revenge*, 58). In "The Pedlar's Revenge" a man tricks his lifelong enemy, a glutton, into eating candles by frying them (as "bacon") with potatoes; like

"Patsa," this story contains a strongly scatological streak. A beggar sings the praises of a would be high-society man in "Your Honour," thereby playing him as an easy mark and getting money from him. Edward Garnett was probably right in rejecting "Colic," yet another early farce, a light-comic vignette set in a pub. O'Flaherty was fond enough of "The Stolen Ass," a comic peasant's ludicrous courtroom attempt to talk his way around the facts surrounding his theft, to read it on his 1978 album in flat, laconic tones. This story is a kind of rural version of Myles na gCopaleen/Flann O'Brien/Brian O'Nolan's comic vignettes set "In the District Court" in his *Irish Times* "Cruiskeen Lawn" column. So is "The Bath," a humorous account of a hungover barrister's feat of getting cleaned up in a hotel a hundred miles from Dublin and delivered to his courtroom in Dublin on time.

O'Flaherty's lighthearted animal stories show that the naturalistic perspective was by no means his only way of looking at animals. "The Jealous Hens" is nearly a low-comic version of "The Wounded Cormorant," in which the hen favored by the cock is terrorized by the other hens (with ridiculous rather than tragic results). Other animal stories bring in people as comic objects. "The Bladder" concerns a cow that drinks too much water and forces its unpopular owner, a schoolmaster, out of farming altogether, but not before this man is branded with the nickname of "the bladder." Another unfortunate is the Aran sanitary officer in "A Pig in a Bedroom," who is unable to send off his government report about the pig because he is constantly assailed by his wife and numerous fawning peasants seeking favors. However, Mr. Edwards in "The Old Hunter," who was sold a racehorse that is apparently an old bag of bones, has the last laugh when he starts winning, proving that there is "something in a pedigree" (*Short Stories*, 143).

Better described as broad social comedies are such stories as "At the Forge" (1925), "An Ounce of Tobacco" (1927), "Mackerel for Sale" (1927), "King of Inishcam" (1935), "Timoney's Ass" (1947), and "The Post Office" (1954). These are O'Flaherty's warmest comedies and include his two best ones, "The Post Office" and "King of Inishcam." Yet five of these six stories were not included in the 1937 or 1956 collections, the only exception being "The Post Office." While his very early low-comic stories disprove the impression that comedy was a dilatory feature in O'Flaherty's career, the comparatively later dates attached to this final group of stories show that it may be fair to say that his humor improved as time passed. Doyle felt that "The Post Office" was "much more in the manner of Frank O'Connor than of

Liam O'Flaherty" (114), and as I noted earlier in the case of "Patsa; or, the Belly of Gold," some of the narrators of O'Flaherty's comic stories recall O'Connor's. These stories are not imitations of O'Connor, however. Rather, they indicate that O'Flaherty was more versatile in style and point of view than has generally been appreciated. Here he departs from his famously visual, naturalistic style in favor of much more frequent use of dialogue and first-person narration. In "At the Forge" Keegan, the keeper of the forge, shows up two hours late for work after having won a fight, for which he is applauded. "An Ounce of Tobacco" recounts a village's mania over tobacco, during wartime rationing, after they learn that a small amount has appeared at the shop. "They are presumably still waging war over that ounce of tobacco, even though the Great War in Europe has long since finished."[81] "Galway Bay" (1939) is an excellent story that focuses on a defiant old man taking the family cow on the steamer from Inis Mór to be sold in Galway. This one is not really a comic story, but it does exemplify (like "The Old Woman") the older O'Flaherty's increased attention to old age.

"King of Inishcam" is a highly entertaining and interesting story that was not anthologized until it appeared in Kelly's 1976 collection of neglected O'Flaherty stories. Like Frank O'Connor's celebrated story "The Majesty of the Law," it focuses on a rural policeman best able to enforce the law only according to the more traditional, deep-rooted values of the lawbreaker and his community. If there was any influence at work here, it was O'Flaherty's on O'Connor, for "King of Inishcam" was first published in a different version and under a different title, "Irish Pride," in 1926, several years before O'Connor's story appeared; O'Connor's review of O'Flaherty (excerpted in part 3) is filled with admiration. More likely, though, the two writers independently picked up on closely similar cultural curiosities. "King of Inishcam" most strongly calls to mind "The Majesty of the Law" when the "king" of the island, after losing his fight with the policeman, walks into the barracks under his own power to sign papers swearing that he will not operate illegal stills anymore. Sean McKelvey is "king" only because his grandfather, when asked in English by policemen if he was in charge of the island—since he was the only one around because everyone else was in hiding during their search for illegal liquor—nodded yes (knowing not a word of English). The first-person narrator of this story, Policeman Corrigan, gradually realizes that he can best gain control over the island not by defeating McKelvey, but rather by allowing him to exercise his authority as "king." Corrigan finally accuses Mc-Kelvey of allowing his men to replace his destroyed still—so that McKelvey can order them not to do so and thus reassert his supremacy. They shake hands: "I do believe that I never have felt so happy in my life as when I grasped the hand of that magnificent man. Nor did I ever afterwards, during my service in the district, have the least trouble with poitheen making on Inishcam" (*Pedlar's Revenge*, 174).

"Timoney's Ass" tells the similar story of the attempt by police to punish a maker of illicit whiskey by repeatedly imprisoning his donkey. Only when rebellion on the mainland forces the police to leave the island does the illegal whiskey trade stop, under the far more effective prohibition of the parish priest. Timoney loses his business and dies, his ass remaining alive and liberated, braying triumphantly on the mountainside. "Mackerel for Sale," though short on plot, is a kind of prototype of "The Post Office," broadly and humorously picturing several amusing character types.

Like "King of Inishcam" and "Timoney's Ass," "The Post Office" draws much of the richness of its comedy from the juxtaposition of insiders and outsiders, Irish speakers and English speakers, natives and foreigners. This story also serves as a comic afterword to O'Flaherty's more frequently heated opinions about the Irish language and bilingualism. Versions of it in English and Irish ("Oifig on Phoist") were both published in 1953, leaving unsettled the question of which version was composed first. It is hilarious in both languages, and is better read than paraphrased. The story involves the exchanges that ensue when a flashily dressed threesome—a fluent Irishman accompanied by American and Spanish women—arrive at the post office in the Irish-speaking village of Praiseach ("Here it must be admitted that the word *praiseach* is Gaelic for confusion, disorder and shapelessness" [*Stories*, 406]). Especially since he is "dressed like a Breton fisherman" (381), the visiting Irishman (who is bemused by all that he witnesses) appears to be the image of O'Flaherty himself, who described his life in Brittany in *Shame the Devil*. The three visitors want to send a telegram to the Spaniard's friend in Los Angeles, but the postmaster is hard pressed to reach Galway in order to send it, engages in various amusing conversations on the phone while ostensibly trying to do so, and (like everyone else in the post office) is too distracted by the visitors to stay on task. When she sees their red-painted toenails, an old woman is convinced that the American and Spanish women are dying. The visiting Irishman confirms her worst fears: "'They are rotting, all right,' said the young man gravely, 'and I'll tell you how that happened. The two of them were imprisoned by savages in a Brazilian forest, near the source of a river called the Amazon. Two years they were kept there and rats were all they had to eat. That's how they caught the dreadful disease that's making them rot slowly, inch by inch.' . . . 'Mother of God!' the hag whispered in horror . . . She made the Sign of the Cross on her bosom, got to her feet as fast as she could and made for the door" (392–93). The Spaniard recites Lorca in Spanish and is warmly applauded by the assembled Irish-speaking throng. Eventually the scene degenerates into an anarchic babble.

"The Post Office" is, on the one hand, O'Flaherty's best comic story and, on the other hand, just one of quite a number of such stories that he wrote. It violates almost every part of the formula for the supposedly "typical" O'Flaherty story: it is funny rather than tragic, long instead of short, diffuse rather than focused, filled with dialogue rather than limited to physical description and action. Only in its faithfulness to Irish rural ways and its use of bilingualism does it look like a "typical" O'Flaherty story. One might indeed wish that O'Flaherty had written more stories like it or as good as it. At the same time, "The Post Office" is just another reminder that there is no single formula for his stories, and that the man who wrote both "The Cow's Death" and "The Post Office" (to name just two of his best stories) was nothing if not capable of an impressive range of short fiction.

Conclusion

O'Flaherty emerges more and more as a very important writer. George O'Brien is not alone in feeling that "it is generally agreed that O'Flaherty is the greatest Irish short-story writer" and that his work guarantees him a "place in the history of modernism."[82] Brendan Kennelly perhaps puts it best when he writes that while "O'Flaherty probably has more faults than any of the other outstanding Irish writers of short stories," at the same time "with the exception of Joyce, he also rises to greater heights. His failures as a writer are directly connected to his ecstatic successes. He is a poet who has chosen to tell stories" (187). O'Flaherty's stories are well worth reading in conjunction with the stories of Joyce's *Dubliners*, for in general they could not be much more different (while equally Irish and modernist).

Until we have a definitive biography of O'Flaherty, there will remain the tenacious and frequently asked question of why, especially considering the prolific nature of his writing in the 1920s and 1930s, O'Flaherty became virtually silent as a creative writer during the last 30 years of his life (and refused to answer questions about his work). The most satisfactory critical answer so far has been a psychoanalytic one. Both Vivian Mercier and Patrick Sheeran have suggested that when the psychically embattled O'Flaherty finally achieved comparative contentment and security in Dublin in the early 1950s, he lost his reason to write; he no longer required the therapy of it.[83] As we have seen, he had been shellshocked in World War I and was always torn between the simple but difficult natural environment of Aran and the wider world. Sheeran writes, "His fear of insanity was . . . an important stimulus to artistic activity. In later life he grew to be more stable: gentleness replaced violence and with it came an end to his creative work" (67).

More simply, it may be that O'Flaherty felt that he had written himself out and could live comfortably on his royalties for the rest of his life. Given his early declaration in "Writing in Gaelic" (1927) that "I write to please myself and two friends . . . my wife and . . . Edward Garnett," and considering that O'Flaherty's storytelling was rooted originally in the oral culture of Inis Mór, it may also be that he felt that he could now retire from the printed page to the intimate, spoken storytelling and conversation enjoyed over drinks with family and friends at home and in the pub. There he could savor a fuller appreciation of his contentious and complex personality than could ever be found in the public arena. This is not to suggest that he simply became mellow and quiet, however, for Tomás de Bhaldraithe assures me that in the 1950s "I knew him and . . . at that time he sometimes came to blows over an argument!"[84] A conclusive answer to this last question—why did O'Flaherty stop writing?—may well remain the most elusive one among the vexing set of problems posed by this surprisingly multifarious author of supposedly "simple" stories. To return to the unfashionable word with which I began, O'Flaherty was first of all a peasant—sometimes servile, often insolent—and like every native of the Aran Islands I ever met, he was anything but uncomplicated.

Notes to Part 1

1. *Shame the Devil* (1934; reprint, Dublin, Wolfhound Press, 1981), 45; hereafter cited in text as *Shame*.

2. The tongue-in-cheek nature of O'Flaherty's attitude toward biography and autobiography is also suggested by the autobiographical excerpts reprinted at the beginning of part 2.

3. Paul A. Doyle, *Liam O'Flaherty* (New York: Twayne, 1971), 7.

4. John Broderick, "The Finest Irish Novelist of His Prolific Generation," *Irish Times*, 22 November 1984, 7; letter to author of 30 September 1988 by Breandán Ó hEithir.

5. *The Life of Tim Healy* (London: Jonathan Cape, 1927), 5; hereafter cited in text as *Healy*.

6. Biographical accounts can be found in John Zneimer, *The Literary Vision of Liam O'Flaherty* (Syracuse, N.Y.: Syracuse University Press, 1970), 1–58; Doyle, *Liam O'Flaherty*, 17–25; James H. O'Brien, *Liam O'Flaherty* (Lewisburg, Penn.: Bucknell University Press, 1973), 15–34; Patrick F. Sheeran, *The Novels of Liam O'Flaherty: A Study in Romantic Realism* (Atlantic Highlands, N.J.: Humanities Press, 1976), 13–111; and my own *Great Hatred, Little Room: The Irish Historical Novel* (Syracuse, N.Y.: Syracuse University Press, 1983), 134–40; all these works are hereafter cited in text. Zneimer's and Doyle's accounts are notable as the earliest in these first critical books on O'Flaherty; Zneimer is best on O'Flaherty's early career as a young writer in Dublin, and Doyle on particular biographical and political details. Sheeran offers the most detail about the Irish context for O'Flaherty's work.

7. "Autobiographical Note," *Ten Contemporaries, Second Series*, ed. John Gawsworth (London: Joiner and Steele, 1933), 143.

8. Original manuscript letter of O'Flaherty to Garnett, dated 28 November 1923, in the O'Flaherty Collection at the Harry Ransom Humanities Research Center of the University of Texas at Austin. All subsequently quoted letters (dated parenthetically in the text) are from this collection.

9. Sheeran's book is the only one devoted specifically to O'Flaherty's novels, while my *Great Hatred, Little Room: The Irish Historical Novel* includes a chapter ("Liam O'Flaherty's Natural History," 133–53) devoted to his historical novels in which *Famine* is singled out for particularly high praise.

10. "Terror" is the title on a manuscript in the O'Flaherty Collection at

the Harry Ransom Humanities Research Center at the University of Texas at Austin.

11. "Irish Revival Delights Liam O'Flaherty," *Irish Press*, 13 May 1946, 4, which is reprinted in part 2 of this book; hereafter cited in text as "Revival."

12. "Writing in Gaelic," *Irish Statesman* 9 (17 December 1927): 348, which is reprinted in part 2 of this book; hereafter cited in text as "Gaelic."

13. Breandán Ó hEithir, "Liam Ó Flatharta agus a Dhúchas" [Liam O'Flaherty and his heritage], in *Willie the Plain Pint—Agus an Pápa* [Willie the plain pint—and the pope] (Dublin and Cork: Cló Mercier, 1977), 68, 70; hereafter cited in text as *Willie*.

14. Conrad Arensberg, *The Irish Countryman: An Anthropological Study* (Gloucester, Mass.: Peter Smith, 1959), 91.

15. *A Tourist's Guide to Ireland* (London: Mandrake, 1929), 109, 132, 133; hereafter cited in text.

16. "Ag Casadh le Pádraic Ó Conaire" (On meeting Pádraic Ó Conaire), *Comhar* (Cooperation) 12 (April 1953): 3–6.

17. See my book *The Irish Novel: A Critical History* (Boston: Twayne, 1988), 116–19, for a sketch of Ó Conaire's remarkable career.

18. Quoted in Tomás de Bhaldraithe, "Ó Flaitheartaigh agus Léirmheastóirí Eile" (O'Flaherty and other critics), *Irish Times*, 22 November 1984, 10; hereafter cited in text as de Bhaldraithe, *Times*.

19. "Death of Liam O'Flaherty Aged 88," *Irish Times*, 8 September 1984, 1; hereafter cited in text as "Death."

20. "*An Braon Broghach*" (The dirty drop), *Comhar* 8 (May 1949): 5, 30.

21. A. A. Kelly, *Liam O'Flaherty the Storyteller* (London: Macmillan, 1976), 129; hereafter cited in text. As invaluable as Kelly's book is, it betrays her self-confessed lack of knowledge of Irish. Her extensive bibliographical listing of the periodical and book appearances of O'Flaherty's stories (145–49) omits his stories in Irish (seven of whose original periodical appearances are separately listed by her on page 142). Two other stories in Irish that are listed—"Briseann an Dúchas" (Nature wins out), *Irish Press*, 30 May 1946, 2, which is actually a version of "An Luchóg" ("The Mouse" as also published in English); and "Throideadar go Fíochmhar" (They fought furiously), *Irish Press*, 6 June 1946, 2, a version of "An Chearc Uisce" ("The Water Hen" as also published in English)—are misfiled by Kelly (142) under "Essays and Letters," mistranslated, and (in the case of "Throideadar") misspelled (as "Throideamar," which is why she mistakenly records that part of the translation as "We Fought"). Another example of the caution one must exercise when a critic who does not know Irish risks a statement about writing in Irish is James F. Kilroy's misreading, in *The Irish Short Story: A Critical History* (Boston: Twayne, 1984), of Tomás de Bhaldraithe and Maureen Murphy's articles: Kilroy claims that both suggest that "The Touch" is better than its Irish equivalent "Teangabháil" (103), whereas in fact they argue just the opposite.

22. Declan Kiberd, *Synge and the Irish Language* (Totowa, N.J.: Rowman and Littlefield, 1979), 5.

23. See, for example, Breandán Ó Buachalla, "Ó Cadhain, Ó Céileachair, Ó Flaithearta," *Comhar* 25 (May 1967): 69–73; Proinsias Ó Cuagáin, "Dúil san Ainmhí: Téama i Scéalta Liam Ó Flaithearta" (Desire in the animal: A theme in Liam O'Flaherty's stories), *Irisleabhar Mha Nuad* (Maynooth Journal) (1968): 49–55, 57–59; Pádraic Breatnach, *Nótaí ar "Dúil"* (Notes on *Dúil*) (Cork: Cló Mercier, 1971); and Fiachra Ó Dubhthaigh, *Léargas ar "Dúil" Uí Fhlaithearta* (Insight into O'Flaherty's *Dúil*) (Dublin: Foilseacháin Náisiúnta, 1981). A good overview of O'Flaherty's place in the tradition of story writing in Irish can be found in an article in English by Maureen Murphy, "The Short Story in Irish," *Mosaic: a Journal for the Comparative Study of Literature and Ideas* 12, no. 3 (1979): 81–89.

24. *The Wounded Cormorant and Other Stories* (New York: Norton, 1973), 44; hereafter cited in text as *Cormorant*. It is a selection out of *The Stories of Liam O'Flaherty* (New York: Devin-Adair, 1956); hereafter cited in text as *Stories*. All parenthetical dates next to titles of stories (and other works) in my text refer to the original publication date of the stories, many of which first appeared in periodicals.

25. For example, Paul Doyle (*Liam O'Flaherty*, 132–34, note 14) cites information from O'Flaherty's sister Delia Ó hEithir (Breandán Ó hEithir's mother) and her husband Pádraic about which language each of the stories in *Dúil* was written in first, but the Ó hEithirs' information was clearly sometimes unreliable: for example, Doyle reports that they said that "Poor People" was written first in English even though O'Flaherty himself wrote to Garnett in July 1925 that it was drafted first in Irish, and they indicated that "An Fiach" (The hunt) and "An tAonach" (The fair) were written first in English even though both stories were published only in Irish, never in English. The best listing of the stories' appearances in Irish and English can be found in William Daniels, "Introduction to the Present State of Criticism of Liam O'Flaherty's Collection of Short Stories: *Dúil*," *Éire-Ireland* 23, no. 2 (Summer 1988): 123–24, note 5. Since writing this chapter I have read Daniels's subsequent article "The Diction of Desire: Liam O'Flaherty's *Dúil*," *Éire-Ireland* 24, no. 4 (Winter 1989): 75–88, which focuses usefully (and quite differently than my own bilingual emphasis) on the patterns of repeated diction in the Irish text of the story.

26. *Adelphi*, 3 (25 September 1925): 258–60.

27. de Bhaldraithe, letter to author of 8 November 1988.

28. Cormac Breathnach, *Field and Fair: Travels with a Donkey in Ireland, Translated from the Irish of Pádraic Ó Conaire by Cormac Breathnach* (Dublin and Cork: Talbot Press, 1929), 33–37.

29. My texts are taken from *Dúil* (Dublin: Sáirséal agus Dill, 1953), 85–90, hereafter cited in text; and from *The Short Stories of Liam O'Flaherty* (1937;

reprint, Kent, England: New England Library, 1986), 161–64, hereafter cited in text as *Short Stories*.

30. Tomás de Bhaldraithe, "Liam O'Flaherty—Translator (?)," *Éire-Ireland* 3, no. 2 (Summer 1968): 149–53, hereafter cited in text as "Translator"; Maureen O'Rourke Murphy, "The Double Vision of Liam O'Flaherty," *Éire-Ireland* 8, no. 3 (Fall 1973): 20–25.

31. *Liam O'Flaherty Reads "The Ecstasy of Angus" and Three Short Stories: "Dúil," "Red Barbara," and "The Stolen Ass"* is a two-disk album, CCT 15 and 16, released in 1978 by Ceirníní Cladaigh with album notes by Richard Ryan.

32. The original Irish here is as follows: "Mo léan géar! Nuair a bhuail sé isteach imeasc an tsolais lonraigh ba léir dá shúile scanraithe nach raibh rud ar bith ina sheasamh ar an aer. Ní raibh aon tuairisc feasta ar an gcuirtín glégeal a mheall é le áilleacht a chuid seod" (*Dúil*, 13).

33. Such is de Bhaldraithe's thesis in "Liam O'Flaherty—Translator (?)." On the other hand, it should be added that at other points O'Flaherty did attempt to preserve the Irish language very literally in his English. As James Stewart notes in "Three Anglo-Irish Notes" (*Occasional Papers 1976–77*, ed. Graham D. Caie et al. [Copenhagen: Akademisk Forlag, 1978], 175), he reproduced the nonsense animal call "seabhnín" as "chowin, chowin, poor chowin" in "Three Lambs" (and also, I might add, in "The New Suit"). Stewart points out that O'Flaherty "must be the first to represent the call in English" and "to use the Irish form in a work of fiction" (175). This is bilingualism carried to the limit—a fragment of one language transliterated in the other.

34. The original Irish is: "Anois níor chuir an teangabháil thobann leis an urlár cruaidh fonn screadaigh air in aon chor. Bhí an oiread sin samhnais ar a chroí, ó bheith ag breathnú ar an gcuirtín seodach lena shúile mó leata, nár thug sé aon aird ar an bpian. D'fhan sé mar sin ar aghaidh an iontais, nó gur neartaigh a dhúil chomh mór sin nach raibh adhradh a shúl i ndon a shásamh. Thosaigh sé ag tnúthán, idir anam agus chorp, le gabháil i dteannta leis an áilleacht. D'ardaigh sé suas é féin ar a lámha agus a ghlúine, le mórchaitheamh tola agus nirt. Sháith sé amach a chlab íochtarach go cróga agus rinne sé ar an gcuirtín solais go díocasach. Níor thug sé iarracht riamh roimhe sin ar lámhacán a dhéanamh" (*Dúil*, 12).

35. The original Irish is: "Chaith a mháthair uaithi an leabhar agus rith sí chuige go mear. Thóg sí suas idir lámha é agus í á phógadh go ceanúil. Choinnigh sé air ag béiciú fad bhí sí á thabhairt sall go dtí an chathaoir. Níor tháinig aon fhoighid ann nó gur shuigh sí síos agus é ar a hucht aici. Nuair a thosaigh sí ag crónán os íseal agus á bhogadh go réidh anonn agus anall, d'imigh an t-uafás de agus is gearr go raibh sé ina thost. Phioc sí suas an gligín ansin den urlár agus chraith sí é amach roimhe. Rinne sé meangadh beag gáire agus rug sé ar an deis torainn ina dhá láimh. Thosaigh sé á chraitheadh. Anseo le taobh na bruinne ina bhfuair sé an beo ní raibh aon bheann aige ar phian ná ar

chontúirt an tsaoil. Anois ba hé glór binn a mháthar bhí á chur faoi dhraíocht; ach go raibh an mealladh seo ciúin agus cineálta. Scuabadh glan amach as a mheabhair cuimhne ar an dochar a d'fhulaing sé agus é ag déanamh mórthriail go doras an domhain. Tháinig samhnas air agus leisce. Shín sé amach a chosa go righin, lig sé osna fada agus theann sé isteach go dlúth le corp teolaí a mháthar. Thosaigh sé ag taibhreamh agus a shúile móra gorma lánoscailte" (*Dúil*, 14–15).

36. The original Irish is: "Nuair a dhún sé a shúile faoi dheireadh agus é ag titim ina chodladh, bhí sé ag craitheadh le dúil in aistear eile a thabhairt amach ón mbroinn, tríd an domhan an bhí taobh thiar den chuirtín lonrach, aistear i ndiaidh aistir, go deireadh a bheatha chorpartha, ag comh-líonadh dualgais an chine dhaonna, le eagla agus doilíos agus áthas, trí ghairdíní bláthacha agus gleannta iargúlta, go dtí beanna na sliabh ag bun na spéire agus suas as sin, nó go seasfadh sé os comhair súile Dé" (*Dúil*, 15).

37. *Evening News* (London), 2 November 1948, 2; *The Bell* 19 (July 1954): 48–50.

38. Tom O'Flaherty's *Aranmen All* (London: Hamish Hamilton, 1934) contains a chapter entitled "My First Suit" (76–82) that narrates essentially the same experience described in "My New Suit," suggesting that it was partly the source for it. Tom O'Flaherty's crucial influence is also suggested by Liam's recollection in "My Life of Adventure" (*T. P.'s Weekly*, 20 October 1928, 756) that even before he stayed with "Miss Casey" in London, "I called on my brother in Boston. He got me a typewriter and told me to write. I wrote some awful stuff." "An Culaith Nua" is a story that disproves Máirtín Ó Cadhain's claim in *Páipéir Bhána, Páipéir Bhreaca* (White papers and speckled papers) that "D'fhéadfadh duine Liam Ó Flatharta a léamh as éadan a chéile gan tagairt ar bith ar éigin don chineál sin saoil" (9, One could read Liam O'Flaherty straight through without reference at all to that kind of life [by which Ó Cadhain means the folklore and folkways of the west of Ireland]).

39. "Sinclair Lewis's *Free Air*," *Irish Statesman* 2 (5 April 1924): 116.

40. "Maupassant's *A Life*," *Irish Statesman* 2 (7 June 1924): 404.

41. John Jordan, *Irish Times*, 8 September 1984, 7.

42. *Two Years* (London: Jonathan Cape, 1930), 14; hereafter cited in text.

43. *Irish Statesman* 6 (8 May 1926): 231–22.

44. *A Cure for Unemployment* (London: E. Lahr, 1931); hereafter cited in text as *Cure*.

45. *I Went to Russia* (New York: Harcourt, 1931), 10.

46. See my *Great Hatred, Little Room: The Irish Historical Novel*, 142–44, for an account of Connolly's influence on O'Flaherty and his historical novels.

47. *Esquire*, May 1942, 120–22.

48. "Unity in Ireland in Year Forecast—Liam O'Flaherty, Author, Here, Sees Early End of Partition of the Ulster Area," *New York Times*, 9 February 1940, 4.

49. "Liam O'Flaherty Ends a Long Life of Many Diverse Roles," *Irish Times*, 8 September 1984, 7.

50. James Joyce, *A Portrait of the Artist as a Young Man* (1916; reprint, New York: Viking / Penguin, 1964), 215.

51. See Terry Eagleton, "Mutations of Critical Ideology," in his *Criticism and Ideology: A Study in Marxist Literary Theory* (Atlantic Highlands, N.J.: Humanities Press, 1976), 11–43, as well as "The Rise of English" in his *Literary Theory: An Introduction* (Minneapolis: University of Minnesota Press, 1978), 17–53.

52. *Joseph Conrad: An Appreciation* (London: Lahr, 1930).

53. Quoted in Terry Eagleton, *Criticism and Ideology*, 139.

54. "Irish Housekeeping," *New Statesman and Nation* 9 (8 February 1936): 186.

55. Benedict Kiely, "Liam O'Flaherty: A Story of Discontent," *Month* 2, no. 5 (September 1949): 184.

56. Sandra Gilbert and Susan Gubar, *The War of the Words*, vol. 1 of *No Man's Land: The Place of the Woman Writer in the Twentieth Century* (New Haven: Yale University Press, 1988); and Declan Kiberd, *Men and Feminism in Modern Literature* (New York: St. Martin's, 1985).

57. Gender is an issue rarely dealt with in previous O'Flaherty criticism. Angeline Kelly remarks briefly on the subject, but the only previous substantive commentary focused on gender is a four-page piece accessible only to readers of Irish: "Mná" (Women) in Fiachra Ó Dubhthaigh's pamphlet on *Dúil* (cited above in note 23), in which he argues that O'Flaherty's women characters tend to be simplistic and stereotypical and that Máirtín Ó Cadhain's fiction was superior in this regard.

58. "Mr. Tasker's Gods," *Irish Statesman* 3 (7 March 1925): 827.

59. "My Life of Adventure," *T. P.'s Weekly*, 20 October 1928, 756.

60. Gearóid Denvir, "The Living Tradition: Oral Irish Language Poetry in Connemara Today," *Éire-Ireland* 24, no. 1 (Spring 1989): 99, 107.

61. *Short Stories* (Dublin: Wolfhound, 1986), 187. Originally published by Wolfhound in 1976 as *The Pedlar's Revenge and Other Stories*; hereafter cited in text as *Pedlar's Revenge*.

62. *The Mountain Tavern and Other Stories* (New York: Harcourt, Brace, 1929), 192; hereafter cited in text as *Tavern*.

63. *Two Lovely Beasts* (1948; reprint, New York: Devin-Adair, 1950), 138.

64. *Spring Sowing* (London: Cape, 1924), 236.

65. *The Ecstasy of Angus* (1931; reprint, Dublin: Wolfhound, 1978), 25.

66. Sheeran, *Novels of Liam O'Flaherty*, 63; Kiely, "Liam O'Flaherty: A Story of Discontent," 185.

67. Ben Forkner, "Modern Irish Short Fiction," in *Critical Survey of Short Fiction: Essays 407–818*, vol. 2, ed. Frank N. Magill (Englewood Cliffs, N. J.: Salem Press, 1981), 670.

68. Charles Walcutt, *American Literary Naturalism, a Divided Stream* (Minneapolis: University of Minnesota Press, 1956), 20. Perhaps because American fiction writers, like the Irish, were in many ways more open to the influence of European naturalist writers than the English were, much of the best critical work on naturalism focuses on the Americans. It is also worth reading John C. Conder's amendment of Walcutt in *Naturalism in American Fiction: The Classic Phase* (Lexington: University Press of Kentucky, 1984).

69. Ernest Hemingway, *Death in the Afternoon* (New York: Scribner's 1932), 122.

70. Seán Ó Faoláin, "Don Quixote O'Flaherty," *London Mercury* 37 (December 1937): 173; excerpted in part 3 of this book.

71. Helene O'Connor, "Liam O'Flaherty: Literary Ecologist," *Éire-Ireland* 7, no. 2 (Summer 1972): 47; excerpted in part 3 of this book.

72. Deborah Averill, *The Irish Short Story from George Moore to Frank O'Connor* (Washington, D.C.: University Press of America, 1982), 129.

73. Quoted by Proinsias Ó Cuagáin (see note 23), 49.

74. O'Flaherty privately derided this story to Garnett: "That's the kind of tripe the public likes. They call it literature" (13 September 1923).

75. John Crawford, "Liam O'Flaherty's Black and White World," *Irish Press*, 1 August 1953, 4.

76. Brendan Kennelly, "Liam O'Flaherty: The Unchained Storm. A View of His Short Stories," in *The Irish Short Story*, ed. Patrick Rafroidi and Terence Brown (Gerrards Cross, England: Colin Symthe; Atlantic Highlands, N.J.: Humanities Press, 1979), 187; excerpted in part 3 of this book.

77. Vivian Mercier, *The Irish Comic Tradition* (Oxford: Clarendon, 1962), 49.

78. A critic such as John Zheimer, while usefully focusing on one side of O'Flaherty (which Zneimer calls existentialism), neglects other leading aspects of his work such as comedy, not even mentioning "The Post Office" in his book. Doyle lists, but does not discuss, O'Flaherty's most strongly satiric monographs, *A Tourist's Guide to Ireland* and *A Cure for Unemployment*.

79. Arthur Pollard, *Satire* (London: Methuen, 1970), 1.

80. Stephen Greenblatt, *Three Modern Satirists: Waugh, Orwell, and Huxley* (New Haven: Yale University Press, 1965), 106.

81. *T. P.'s Weekly*, 8 October 1927, 740.

82. George O'Brien, in *Novelists and Prose Writers*, ed. James Vinson (London: Macmillan, 1979), 927; excerpted in part 3 of this book.

83. Vivian Mercier, "Man against Nature: The Novels of Liam O'Flaherty," *Wascana Review* 1, no. 2 (1966): 44–45 (excerpted in part 3); Sheeran, *Novels of Liam O'Flaherty*, 67.

84. Letter to author of 24 October 1989, quoted with Professor de Bhaldraithe's kind permission.

Part 2

THE WRITER

Introduction

Reprinted in this section are excerpts from a number of articles and letters by O'Flaherty. For the most part these sources are either published here for the first time (in the case of most of the selections from his letters to Edward Garnett) or otherwise generally very difficult to obtain. They offer a wide range of invaluable perspectives on this writer's life, personality, writing career, politics, views of art and culture, and opinions on the Irish language and other themes explored in my own critical chapters.

Selections from three autobiographical essays by O'Flaherty shed light on the centrality of the Aran Islands to his view of the world, and the first excerpt reflects both the writer's diverse early life experiences and his sense of humor. His letters to Garnett are introduced by his own comments about Garnett and are grouped under a series of thematic headings: the mentor relationship, nature, the reading public, the literary marketplace, comedy, Dublin, and story writing. In his biography of Garnett, H. E. Bates wrote that "O'Flaherty had arrived in London with a firebrand swagger, a fine talent and headful of rebellious fury about the English and had sat down to write pieces of episodic violence about London, which he hardly knew at all. Garnett promptly and rightly sent him back to Ireland to write about seagulls and congers, a peasant's cow and the flight of the blackbird, and he at once produced sketches of the most delicate feeling and visual brilliance that few, even among the Irish, have equalled."[1]

O'Flaherty advanced his critique of art and culture in several letters, reviews, and articles in such periodicals as the *Irish Statesman* in the 1920s and early 1930s, and several of these are included here. In them he champions passion, tumult, and indigenous culture, and attacks censorship. (Unlike many other Irish fiction writers, O'Flaherty himself was censored less than one might expect, probably mostly because those books of his that would have most raised the censors' hackles, such as *The Black Soul* and *Mr. Gilhooley*, were published before the passage of the Censorship of Publications Act of 1929.) His preface to his *Life of Tim Healy* is excerpted here largely because it is one of his funniest pieces of writing.

The final selections in this section are O'Flaherty's very bitter 1927 letter in the *Irish Statesman* about writing in Irish and the sharply contrasting 1946 *Irish Press* interview entitled "Irish Revival Delights Liam O'Flaherty." This headline reflects the much more positive, nostalgic attitude to the language adopted by the older O'Flaherty, having returned from the United States to Dublin during a period when cultural conditions had become more favorable to writing in Irish. This 1946 piece is also notable more generally as a rare interview granted before the near silence of O'Flaherty's last thirty years from the early 1950s until his death in 1984.

Anyone reading O'Flaherty's letters and other writings will be immediately struck by his lively, cantankerous, yet deceptively complex personality—certainly a major part of trying to understand his life and work. Even contemporaries who knew him fairly well have provided conflicting versions of his temperament. Viewing him as a garrulous Irish character, Bates recalled, "O'Flaherty, true Irish, could talk a donkey's hind leg off and with fierce, blue, unstable eyes would stand up in the middle of the room and begin reciting flowing nonsense from some as yet unwritten book, about 'women pressin' their thighs into the warm flanks of the horses,' until he codded you that it had really happened and was really true."[2] More damning was Seán O'Casey's view of O'Flaherty as a self-serving young ideologue, which is also the best-known comment on his personality because of O'Casey's own fame and the appearance of his remarks about O'Flaherty in his widely read autobiographical volume *Inishfallen, Fare Thee Well* (1949). O'Casey understandably resented O'Flaherty's negative letter in the *Irish Statesman* about his play *The Plough and the Stars* (1926), which is reprinted here immediately following the quotation about it from O'Casey's autobiography, which provides an invaluable if contentious context for O'Flaherty's letter and other contributions to the *Irish Statesman* in the 1920s.

In contrast, Gerald Griffin was convinced that O'Flaherty was in fact more sensitive and complicated than Bates and O'Casey made it seem, noting that "people who only know Liam O'Flaherty from his books or from a superficial acquaintance with him vote him a cynical, dour, and rather sullen and unsociable fellow, just as those who do not know Shaw personally regard him as a kind of Diogenes snarling from his tub. But the converse is actually true of both men." Griffin explained,

"Shaw is a genial and even jovial conversationalist, and Liam O'Flaherty's aloofness with those whom he does not know very well is really a cloak for his extreme shyness. His sympathy with the victims of poverty or illness is profound and often takes a very practical form, and if he hates anything it is cant, humbug, and hypocrisy."[3] Writing on the subject of "Personalities: Liam O'Flaherty" in the *Irish Tatler and Sketch* in 1949, an anonymous columnist who called himself "Nimrod" similarly remarked, "If you go to meet O'Flaherty expecting to encounter a rugged, violent man you will be disappointed. There is about him personally little of the explosive quality of his writing." Sharply contradicting Bates's characterization, "Nimrod" added, "Quiet and urbane, he looks anything but the wild islander. He still preserves the lithe figure of the Aran man, the erect carriage of the ex-guardsman, and his remarkable aquamarine eyes have lost none of the bellicose quality that others have noted in him, none of the 'leppin' on his native rocks and daring all-comers."[4] Like his work, O'Flaherty's character remains more enigmatic than his typically hard, simple public surface would make it seem, and his differing moods are most evident in his letters to Garnett.

Notes

1. H. E. Bates, *Edward Garnett* (London: Max Parrish, 1950), 49.

2. Ibid., 49.

3. Gerald Griffin, "Liam O'Flaherty," *The Wild Geese: Pen Portraits of Famous Irish Exiles* (London: Jarrolds, 1938), 194.

4. "Personalities: Liam O'Flaherty," *The Irish Tatler and Sketch*, April 1949, 36.

Catalog of Life Roles and Experiences

O'Flaherty, Liam. "Life History, so far, of the man known as Liam O'Flaherty: Born Aran Islands, Co. Galway, Ireland, 28th August, 1896. Educated Rockwell College, Blackrock College and University College, Dublin. Joined British Army 1915. Served in France therewith. Discharged with shell-shock, May, 1918. Set out to conquer the world August, 1918, from the Aran Islands. Worked in London as a foreman in a brewery, a porter in a hotel, and as a clerk in an office. Walked out of the office and went to sea as a trimmer on a tramp steamer. Left the steamer at Rio de Janeiro. Didn't like the place. Came back in the same capacity on another steamer to Liverpool. Joined another at Cardiff and went east, to Italy, Turkey, Greece, etc. Thence to Montreal, where he left the ship. Wandered over Canada, working in the capacity of lumberjack, railway worker, tinned milk maler, miner in copper mines, dock labourer, hobo carpenter. Crossed the American frontier without a passport in November, 1919. Joined his brother in Boston. Followed various avocations in various States of the Union, to wit, maker of pastry, telegraph messenger, oyster fisher, house-porter, dish-washer, waiter, in a construction camp boarding-house, dynamite worker in Dupont's works, shipyard worker, plumber's assistant, printer's assistant, rubber tyre maker, and labourer in biscuit factory. Joined another ship at New York, August, 1920, to return to Ireland. Carried to South America instead. Joined another ship at Santos, Brazil, and travelled to Belgium, Holland and Germany thereon. Came from Hamburg to Cardiff. Came to Ireland from Cardiff in November, 1920. Stayed a few weeks in that country and passed to London once more, where he stayed until January, 1921, in which month he returned to the Aran Islands without having conquered any part of the world. Meditated for many months in the aforesaid islands on the indefinability of the paregoric, the uncertainty of life, and the constant tribulations to be met with in this world. Roused himself to a

Reprinted from *The Best Short Stories of 1926*, ed. Edward J. O'Brien (New York: Dodd, Mead, 1927), 406–7.

88

desire for a further attempt at world conquest in August, 1921. Set out for London once more, but returned to Ireland in December of the same year and became active in various manners, to wit, in the organization of the unemployed and the seizure of the Rotunda, over which he hoisted the Red Flag, and fed the poor, in participation in the Four Courts rebellion, and later in a further departure from the scene of these activities by going once more to London, where, in September, 1922, he commenced to write. Since then he has written divers books called: *Thy Neighbour's Wife, The Black Soul, Spring Sowing, The Informer,* and *The Tent*. He is now resident in Glencoe, Co. Wicklow, Ireland, still meditating on the indefinability of the paregoric."

"My Experiences (1896–1923)"

Since the earliest days that I can remember my greatest pleasure in life was wandering in solitude, finding greater pleasure in the companionship of the sea, the wind, animals and birds, and in all nature than in people. As a boy I was continually getting lost and searched for and found and scolded and then getting lost again. Very often they found me sitting in a niche of the gaunt cliffs of Aran listening to the sea. Then I used to dream of tramping all over the world. Just that and nothing more.

When I left Aran at the age of twelve and went to school at Rockwell College in Tipperary, the wanderlust was nurtured by my hatred of being walled in and flogged and forced to learned [sic] Greek and Latin and Algebra. But it was not until I had finished school, matriculated and spent nearly two years in University College, Dublin, that I at last plucked up courage and spread my wings.

My first flight was not very pleasurable. I went into the Irish Guards and soon felt the soul-devouring horror of war, the thunder of deadly guns so different to the beautiful passionate roar of the sea, and the brutalising effect of perpetually cohabiting with ghastly death, hunger and debauched ideals. A kind shell released me in September, 1917, and I returned, soured and disillusioned and prone to sleepless nights, when I lay awake and wanted to compose epic poems about black and horrible things.

Everybody wanted me to choose a respectable means of earning a livelihood after my discharge, but I chose a suitcase, a copy of Shelley's poetry, Haeckel's *Riddle of the Universe,* and the open road. I went to London in September, 1918, and then for the first time in my life I felt really free and happy. One week I was a foreman in a brewery, the next week I was a night-porter in a hotel. The next week I turned down the offer of a job in a musical comedy and became a clerk in a Piccadilly business house. And a fortnight later I got sick of London and joined a tramp steamer bound for Rio De Janeiro as a coal trimmer.

From *Now and Then,* no. 10 (December 1923): 14–15.

Ah, the joy of the first tropical moon on a still sea! And the joy of seeing the first shoal of flying fish!

Then I moved rapidly from Rio to Liverpool, thence to Cardiff, to Alexandria, Salonica, Constantinople, Smyrna, Malta, Gibraltar, Montreal. I covered all Ontario, Manitoba, Quebec, New Brunswick and Nova Scotia. I crossed into the United States and tramped and worked in about twelve states. I embarked again at New York and visited Barbadoes, Pernambuco, Bahia, Rio, Santos, Paranaqua, Rio Grande Do Sul, Montevideo, Antwerp, Rotterdam, Hamburg and Cardiff. Thence I went to Ireland with a bad attack of neurasthenia. The Black and Tan Terror was then at its height in October, 1920. The nature of the contest did not enthuse me, so in spite of my desire to be doing something, I stayed listening to the sea in Aran, a prey to the darkest melancholy, for several months. I think it was then that the desire to write grew upon me. I had written several short stories while in the United States, but merely as a pastime. But while in Aran my mind was perpetually burning with something that boiled within it, and I spent many a long day with a pen and a notebook trying to write something about the sea and unable to write anything.

Then I got disgusted with everything, and came over to London in September, 1921. There I became enthused with Communism and returned to Ireland once more, and my friends and I had dreams of a Soviet republic. The effort resulted in failure. We attempted to sieze Dublin in January, 1922, and did sieze the Rotunda, and held it for three days, feeding about ten thousand unemployed. But the unemployed and the working class greatly resented the idea, and burned our small force out of the building. Until June I persisted in the endeavour to help the masses. Then I joined the Four Courts rising. That finished with, I left for London in September, 1922, and began to write *Thy Neighbour's Wife*.

Apprenticeship as a Writer

I think the first attempt at writing fiction I made was at the age of seven or thereabouts. The schoolmaster of our village school, a most worthy man, asked us all to write a short story. I wrote some hundred words describing the murder of a peasant woman by her husband.

The wife brought him cold tea for dinner to the field. He murdered her with a spade and then tried to bury her in the fosse, or furrow, between two ridges. The point of the story, I remember, was the man's difficulty in getting the woman, who was very large, to fit into the fosse. The schoolmaster was horrified and thrashed me.

Some years later, my brother and I decided to write a novel conjointly. I was then eleven years old I think. But after a few days I quarrelled with him, as I wanted to do it all myself.

At thirteen I was sent away to school, with a view to entering the Church. My brother had been set aside for that profession, but he had already become a Socialist. I don't remember how he became one, but I think it was because we were all Republicans, our family. At that time, there were about one hundred Republicans in Ireland, so we were very bitter. Hearing that the Pope denounced Republicanism and Socialism, my brother became a Socialist. So he refused the clerical profession. Naturally he became an outcast in the district and he had to clear out to the United States.

I remember that the only friend I had when I went to school was an English boy. The other boys disliked him because he was English, and they disliked me because I was a Republican, or a rebel as they called it. I remember that I disliked them thoroughly myself. For that reason I became very studious and at the age of fifteen I was a complete agnostic.

At that time there was a considerable interest in the Gaelic language. I was asked to compete for a gold medal offered by some society in America for an essay in Gaelic. I won the prize with an essay on emi-

Reprinted from "Autobiographical Note," *Ten Contemporaries, Second Series*, ed. John Gawsworth (London: Joiner and Steele, 1933), 139–43.

gration or some such thing. Some years later, while a student in Dublin, I pawned that medal with some others, to buy a revolver, while I was a member of the Republican Army.

A few months after winning the medal for my essay I was sent away from that school for refusing to become a priest. Then I went to another school and was almost expelled from that for organising a corps of Republican Volunteers. That was in 1913. Eoin MacNeill, a professor who was in command of that organisation at the time, sent me a long manifesto authorising me to organise the schoolboys. The schoolboys pelted me and my few comrades with stones around the recreation ground. Some of them are now generals in the Free State Army. However, the authorities of the school did not threaten to expel me for that, as much as for an essay I wrote claiming that Catholicism in the Middle Ages was a mass of superstition and that the idea of nationalism was unChristian, since it was barbarous that a man living on one side of a rock should be asked to kill a man living on the other side. How I managed to act as commander of a corps of schoolboy Republican volunteers and at the same time denounce nationalism I know not.

Next year I went to college, and during my first year I attempted to write a novel, but I got no further than a page or so. They were very exciting times in Dublin. Everybody was enthused with some sort of war mania. I myself was a volunteer in the Republican force and an anarchist. We organised a small group at the college, but it was broken up. And, finally, having grown tired of waiting for a Republican rebellion, I joined the British Army, I think with the intention of deserting to the German Army and fighting with them, because we in Ireland, the Republicans, were then under the delusion that the Germans were fighting for freedom. Principally, I suppose, because the majority of the people supported the British.

In France I met a Scotchman who was a Socialist and he converted me to that faith. Then my outlook on life altogether changed. I was brought in contact there with all manner of working men, French, English, British Colonials and German prisoners with whom we talked both across the trenches and in the internment camps. I attribute the awakening of my conscious mind to this experience. I became bored with Irish Republicanism and have never since evinced any interest in it. I remember a Romish count who was an officer in our regiment. He has since remained one of the great heroes or figures in my life. And I think it was the desire to write a story about him that first really persuaded me to write. He was a splendid fellow, handsome, brave, a notorious drunkard and libertine and a thorough gentleman, as we understand it in Ireland. He and I became great friends. When he got killed I was more melancholy than I have been since over any loss. A little later I myself was sent down the line, having been blown up in a German counter-attack at Langemarck or some such place.

After my discharge from the army I went home to the Aran Islands, and there began to write some short stories which I read to a few friends. They were amused, but they thought nothing of them. Then instead of returning to the University I set off to tramp the world. I was away a few years without anybody knowing my whereabouts, until at last I turned up in Boston, Mass., to see my brother. He got me a typewriter and ordered me to sit down and write. Together we brought my first story to the Four Seas Company in Boston. I never heard what happened to the manuscript, as I persuaded my brother to leave Boston the following week and come tramping with me. He did not go very far. I wrote some more stories while working in a rubber factory in Hartford, Conn., and burned them. I burned them because I was reading Maupassant at the time and found that mine were barbarous compared to those of the great master.

Then I went to South America and did some more wandering, finally coming back to Ireland in 1920 to find them fighting the Black and Tans. The affair did not interest me, as by this time I had become a Communist, so I went over to London and there I again began to write. These efforts I also burned. I returned to Ireland again and became engaged in an effort to start a Communist revolution. I seized a building and hoisted a red flag over it. We held out for some days, but were finally forced to capitulate to some Free State officer. Then I joined the Republican Four Courts Rebellion, and after its failure decided to make a last effort to write something. I had been writing articles for Republican papers like the *Plain People*, but no fiction.

In London, in September, 1922, I began to write definitely, finished one novel in a few weeks, about 150,000 words. At the same time I was writing several short stories a week. None of the stories was printed. The novel was submitted to Allen & Unwin, but they returned it. At least two million people were slaughtered during the course of the story. Three days after I received the returned manuscript I began *Thy Neighbour's Wife*. The typescript of the first novel I sent to America to my brother. He wrote back to say that a novel must be something more than a bar-room story. He still keeps the manuscript and I am unable to burn it.

I remember writing a chapter of *Thy Neighbour's Wife* in a theatre queue waiting to hear Madame Melba. When I had finished it, Mrs. Hamilton suggested my sending it to Cape. I met her by having a story printed in the *New Leader*, my first story printed, one called *The Sniper*. Being hard up I threatened to blow up their office unless they paid me at once. They were very amused.

Cape took the manuscript on the recommendation of Edward Garnett. I met Edward Garnett. He took me in hand and suggested that I should write about animals. In fact, I owe Edward Garnett all I know about the craft and a great deal of all I know about the art of writing. To his kindness, his help, his marvellous critical faculty and his loving friendship I owe whatever success I have had subsequently in creating my work. We practically wrote the *Black Soul* together. I remember his burning about 30,000 words of manuscript upon which I had spent a whole month. I could have shot him. The book, when it appeared, was treated with contempt, although in my own opinion it is much better than *The Informer* which was received very favourably.

Since then I have been writing steadily and living a peaceful life.

The Literary World as a Fortress

I remember Edward Garnett telling me when I began to write that the literary world is like a fortress. Established writers are within, comfortable, with money in their pockets, good wine in their bellies, and with their minds dulled by success. Young writers are roaming about outside in the slums that surround the fortress, consorting with the ruffians . . . of the alley ways. They jeer at those within, hurl stones at them and lampoon them. Those within keep out those without, by every foul means.

Now and again a giant arises and storms the fortress; but that is very rare, for the garrison sees to it that a writer of genius finds it difficult to raise an army of readers.

Reprinted from the foreword to *The Stars, the World, and the Women* by Rhys Davies (London: William Jackson, 1930), 7–9.

Letters to Edward Garnett

Garnett as Mentor

I thank you for getting "The Fight" accepted. This is another strong-hold carried by assault. (17 August 1923)

After I have seen you and have got an outline of the work I should do I'll come here [to Dublin] like an ancient Gaelic warrior going to make an inroad on a Firbolg settlement. (April 1924)

I got your letter this morning and was delighted to hear that you liked the cow. It's not the sketch itself but the fact that at last I know what is wanted to write one that pleases me. Thanks so much for showing me. You see I was always aiming after this damn cleverness in expression without bothering about the bones of the corpse upon which I was operating—probably copying the daily papers, but I imagine the fault is hereditary. However that damn cow like all cows, persisted in coming back from the *Manchester Guardian* last night. Now if I had not known you, I would have torn that up considering it to be a rotten production and only worthy of the basket. But you better not tell me that I am writing too well or I might get a swelled head—it's swelled enough already, and we Irish are very prone to enlarging our area about the neck at the least encouragement or for the lack of it. (5 May 1923)

This morning I see "The Cow's Death" in the *New Statesman*. It reads well in print. Well that's your sketch. You taught me how to write that one. I thank you very much. I have not done anything as good as it since. I don't think "Three Lambs" comes near it. (4 June 1923)

From original letters in the O'Flaherty Collection at the Harry Ransom Humanities Research Center, University of Texas at Austin. Reprinted by permission of the Harry Ransom Humanities Research Center and Peters Fraser & Dunlop Group Ltd.

I am writing a story now, inspired by El Ombu. I started out and wrote it in Irish and then translated it into English, using the phraseology that they would use in Aran. I am telling the truth, so it is surprising what similitude there is between the mode of expression and the Spanish one. "The Black Mare" it's called. I owned the mare myself but I get old Pathcheen Saele to tell it, he was the greatest braggart in Aran.

Say. I am beginning to see the light now—about how to write. I can see that the only thing one can write with any merit is the truth—the things one knows. Thanks. (8 May 1923)

I have done another sketch which I am sending you to examine (I am really a heartless fellow) because there is a fault I think in it, which Salkeld and myself detected and I want to make sure it is a fault. I mean that I think the end is too abrupt. For the rest, I think myself that the sketch is perfect. Now why is the end bad? This is very important for me to find out, because if I do understand it and master that fault, I imagine that I am master of that length of sketch, in that method. I hope you will like the theme and the treatment. . . . One might as well write for the love of the thing. My short stories you see fill that instinct. (July 1925)

I am also sending you two sketches in my *First Best Style* to show you that I am still writing in that style. . . . Neither of course is as good as "The Cow's Death," but I am afraid we must never hope to equal that first breaking of the virgin soil. . . . At the moment, the job is, *short stories, short stories, short stories*. I have done ten in three weeks and I have about thirteen more to do. (16 July 1925)

Finding the Truth in Nature

I sat for two hours in a field yesterday watching young heifers. It's peculiar the way they lie down. Invariably they raise snouts in the air and blow out their breath. I think it's to clear their nostrils. . . . I never noticed this before. . . . I love the country. The wind sighing in the trees is music to me. Say, sometime when I make a lot of money you must come down to the Aran Islands with me. I say when I make a lot of money because assumedly I would have to buy a quart of whiskey for every man in the island. I was just thinking yesterday of the . . . piers at Kilronan in summer, lying with hands beneath the head listening to the boatman curse and talk about the coarse side . . . in a poetic manner, then watch some maiden bathe on the sandy beach. (April 1923)

Hope you are enjoying the cliffs . . . I am greedy about cliffs. Wait though, till you see the "Hill of Slaughter," and "The Yellow Gable," in Aran. They are what you might call cliffs. We will go round in a curragh. (22 June 1923)

I am inclined not to agree with you about the sketch. . . . Unfortunately in real life in Aran . . . the people accept *necessity* without any resistance and there is only a dull mourning and rebellion of the heart. It's curious. I don't think I exert any judgment whatsoever in my writing at the moment of writing but seem to be impelled by the Aran Islanders themselves who cry out dumbly to me to give expression to them, and of course that has the drawback of all instinctive writing, that it appears to be unfinished, just like a natural landscape. You don't know where to put an end to it, or it sometimes ends where it shouldn't end. (31 July 1925)

I am glad you liked the sketches and that you preferred "Prey" to the other one, because I feel that "what is good in itself" should be better than what is good largely by artifice i.e. as a result of applied intelligence, what is commonly and erroneously regarded as the true expression of art. The harder the rock the longer it lasts. The more primitive the stock the longer it takes to become over refined by civilisation. And conscious art is always over refined. The modern short story or sketch seems to have become a poem and where ideas and images attain lordship over poetry it ceases to be elemental and universal. . . . It was splendid in Aran. The island has the character and personality of a mute God. One is awed in its presence, breathing its air. Over it broods an overwhelming sense of great, noble tragedy. The Greeks would have liked it. The people are sadly inferior to the island itself. But the sea birds are almost worthy of it. The great cormorant thrilled me. And while fishing . . . a great bull seal rose from the sea in front of me. He looked at me with brutal drunken eyes and then dived. Father says they have nests there in caves. (17 June 1927)

The Reading Public

This ogre the public . . . refuses to ask "What did he write?" but lasciviously inquires into the colour of the author's pajamas. (12 October 1923)

Isn't it damn ridiculous that artists are not allowed a clean bill of health as a compensation for the insults of the mob? There was a scurrilous article in the *Irish Independent* about me which made me sore. It accused me of seeking notoriety by writing for pornographic papers. It meant *The Adelphi* in which I had a story "The Outcast." Wouldn't Middleton Murray [its editor] love to be called pornographic. (16 February 1925)

The Literary Marketplace

You know there is a lot of work to be done on those stories yet before they are fit for publication. (April 1924)

If he wants to make money on me quick tell him to publish that book of short stories. They go into rhapsodies here about my short stories but they refuse to discuss *Thy Neighbour's Wife*. I have had letters from every publisher in Dublin asking for a collection of short stories after the publication of "Going Into Exile" in the *Dublin Magazine*. . . . Unfortunately nobody in Ireland has enough money to pay more than a pound for a story of two thousand words. And they know nothing atall about the difference between, let us say, a sketch like "The Rockfish" and "Selling Pigs." Of course they would consider "Selling Pigs" much superior. . . . I will write in future for the satisfaction of my own soul since that to me is the most important thing in the world or in the next either. I have reluctantly but finally given up all hope either of being great before I die or of ever making enough money even to pay my debts. (2 May 1924)

Herewith "The Bladder," "The Tramp" and a new story "Colic." Please put "Colic" in the collection. It will be popular in Ireland among the people that buy books. I am also writing "A Pot of Gold" which will be good for the collection. And I will let you have "A Rat Trap" as soon as the *Manchester Guardian* print it. I fancy that all my recent work will bear the mark of the Irish influence and that they are better in the collection than the previous human ones, which had a certain artificial influence. This is purely theoretical, but I fancy that I am in closer touch here with life and am writing with greater discrimination and greater difficulty of admitting a thing as finished, which after all is I suppose a proof that one is more critical.

I will send you "Wolf Lanigan's Death" and "A Day's Madness." I won't send "Fishing" as I think it's not good enough as you say. The other two stories are in AE's office but I am going into town in a few days time and get the office typist to copy them out for me.

The other day a man paid me a great compliment. He said that the only two people who seemed to be able to get the Russian "picture" into their writing were Conrad and myself. Puffed up by such a combination of names I said proudly: "Ah yes, but Conrad and myself studied under the same master." And the man said when I told him who the master was "There ye are, what did I tell you. Wawn't I right."

For me life is very lonely here without you. It seems nobody else is in any way deeply interesting. You see one has a devilish hero worship for a man one allows to throw one's manuscript in the fire. During the past month when I was in agonies trying to find the right way out for my novel I said to myself: "Now if Edward Garnett were here he would tell me in half an hour what I should do and the way would be clear." But maybe it's good for me to have to begin to do these things myself. Although I would like very much if you would be so kind as to read the chapters for me and give your judgment.

"The Wren's Nest" and "The Landing" have been printed last week and in this country "The Hook" was printed, so that as a short story writer I am becoming quite a little success. Maybe after all that I will be able to support myself by writing short stories. The agent is trying to sell some for me in U.S. but they said it would be difficult because the stories "have a literary flavour." What d'ye think of that. I am sending "Colic" to the *Yorkshire Weekly Post* where you advised me to try. I am sending it to the Literary Editor since I do not know your friend's name. "The Wild Sow" was most unpopular in this country. Everybody expressed surprise that I could have written such a coarse and vulgar thing. The Irish national animal, THE PIG, is not popular in print. Inferiority complex again. (9 May 1924)

I really don't know whether a cheap edition of *Spring Sowing* would sell in Ireland. You see there are three stories or four there that would spoil it, "Benedicamus Domino," "Josephine," "Beauty," and "Three Lambs." And it is questionable whether there are sufficient half crowns in Ireland. . . . I am working so hard at my novel that I am not very much interested in anything else. (16 May 1924)

I can't write stories while I am working at my novel. . . . My interest in "pure art" and such trivial matters is not very great. I write my stories as I have to write them, perhaps unfortunately. But I have never written a word yet with my eye on the market. . . . My curse on publishers, editors and the public. To the deepest pit of hell with them. I have a lovely story on hand and I have to rush it off at such a speed, in order to get back to my short stories for some money, that I'm afraid it's going to come a cropper. It won't be as good as it would be otherwise if I could spend an extra month at it. I'm writing about four thousand words a day steadily. (24 January 1926)

I am very glad you liked "The Wave." Very glad indeed. It cost me such an immense effort to write it. But I think I would rather try *The Spectator* with it than the *Manchester Guardian*. None of these young men who review books read the *Manchester Guardian*. (26 January 1926)

Writing Comedy

I guess I am coming near the end of my tether in these sketches—repeating myself and using a fixed formula. I am trying one in the personal style about fishermen. I am not meeting with very much success, but if I get in on it I will have a wide field telling stories about all the funny people and customs in Inverara. (August 1923)

I am enclosing a story which is a new departure in method and in style, to a lesser extent. I wonder what you will think of it. I call it a flippant story. Whether I have succeeded in hiding its flippancy sufficiently under a cloak of art I don't know. I would rather like this method if it could be developed into anything worth while. But one is always looking for new methods and one is never satisfied. (11 April 1924)

I wrote this this morning and am sending it to you for the collection because I think it's worth putting it in instead of some of the other mournful ones. . . . Do you think the ending is weak? I fancy it was impossible to get a dramatic ending under the circumstances. You see it's an incident from life and these incidents from life are generally

more difficult from the point of view of good art than purely imaginative pieces. . . . There is another, "Begging," but it's serious and it
does not enthuse in the present mood, which is humourous. (21 May
1924)

I am vexed that you rejected "Colic" from the collection. I think
you should include it. In fact I must have it included as I consider it
an excellent humourous story. You have a prejudice against humourous
stories. . . . I have a beautiful short story on hand but I am too exhausted to write it. I have begun it. It's glorious. What a delight it is
to be able to write. When I have a writing mood I forget everything
and every unpleasant person and thing that can meet with me. . . . I
know that both these novels will sell on the strength of my short stories.
My short stories will be popular but for myself these two novels will
stand out as far greater and of more spiritual importance than anything
I may do. (23 May 1924)

Making a Mark in Dublin

Let me see now where do we begin. Yes the best place to begin is with
a description of my visit to George Russell yesterday evening. He
keeps open house on Sunday nights and about twenty people gathered
there, people connected with art and literature. Stephens the novelist
was there, a nice fellow enough, but rather proud of himself, denun-
ciatory of the Russians, and very much of the pattern of Robert Lynd,
Squire and those people. We got on well however, which I effected by
keeping my mouth shut and agreeing with him on every point, even
to the extent of saying that Chekhov is very much overrated. Then
there was a Professor Curtiss, expansive, voluble, a writer of ten guinea
reviews for the American Press and a thoroughly hearty fellow. We
talked about the Aran Islands. Then there was Professor Curtiss's wife,
a very pretty young woman, fifteen years younger than the professor.
She has just written a pretty novel, she writes short stories and she
made violent eyes at me. I walked back to Dublin with her, while the
professor followed with another young genius, who combines great personal beauty, a taste in dress, a practice at the Irish bar with a taste for
dabbling in literature. He reviews books. The lady told me all about
her life since the year of her birth, including a description of her private
life, her love affairs and her propensity for falling in love with every
interesting person she met. She would be very valuable to Chekhov.

For the rest there were American journalists, Indian hereditary saints travelling in Ireland (why I don't know) and young poets and women of an indiscriminate type, who just seemed to be connected with the men, like all Irish women just seem to be in public, unless they are very pretty like the professor's wife.

They had all read my book, but none offered to say it was good or bad. One young poet said he liked my stories and hoped that I would collect them and give up novel writing for short story writing and that was all. Still I got on far better than I expected. But there is absolutely nothing doing from a remunerative point of view in the literary field. I must seek elsewhere for a job. They are a pack of scoundrels anyway. I met numbers of people who were asking about my book, but they wanted to borrow a copy. There is not a single copy offered for sale in Dublin. Several people told me they wanted to buy it and couldn't get a copy. . . . Its great fun coming into contact with life again after being so long cooped up with books and silence. Everywhere I am meeting people and talking and watching. Its great fun. I have all sorts of types here in Dublin. One can get peasant types here as fresh as in Connemara.

There is a fine play running at the Abbey Theatre by a man called Sean Casey. He is a friend of mine and I went up this morning to see him. I found him dressed in a suit of dungarees sweeping out a hall where workmen gamble at night. That is his occupation. Fine chap. He is about forty and a nervous wreck like myself. He said he locks himself in at night and then feels happy and very often is afraid to stretch his legs in bed lest he might suffocate. He is also losing his eyesight. We talked about Chekhov and Eugene O'Neill for a long time. He is an artist, unlike the other bastard writers I met here. The play is a fine thing. It is called "Juno and the Paycock." A fine piece of realistic work but in my own opinion he spoils it with tragedy. However. He naively asked me had I made much money on my novel and was dumbfounded when I told him I hadn't. He thought that one had only to write a novel and be rich, unlike writing a drama which only plunges one deeper into poverty. Poor devil.

It is very nice here but I am as far removed from the flesh pots as I was in London I fear. However I am laying a store of impressions and I am living. It appears that we are going to have another revolution here. Some generals are in revolt. Everybody is in a panic. President Cosgrave couldn't get a hearing yesterday at a public meeting. The whole audience hounded him off the platform. (10 March 1924)

These damn short stories have been the cause of more worry to me during the past year than the whole of the great war. . . . Dublin would be a delightful place to live if one had a nice house on the outskirts and a fixed income. It's ideal in every other way except the financial way. I met the editor of the *Dublin Magazine* and he likes my writing very much. He happens to be a Republican of course. I think I may give him "Going Into Exile," but the blighter has no money and he can only pay about a guinea a thousand. I could sell every[thing] I [write] for the next two years in Dublin within twenty four hours, but all I could get would be a guinea a thousand. They pay for politics in this country but they refuse to pay for literature, unless it is political literature. Russell gave me some books to review and I fancy that in about a month's time or so I will be able to rake up enough here and there to keep me in rations. (14 March 1924)

I sold "Going Into Exile" to the *Dublin Magazine*. It will appear in the April number, together with a little Irish sketch of mine. They pay hardly anything but it's good propaganda here. . . . In Ireland where nearly everybody takes himself seriously, it is very easy for a writer to see the silly side of himself. In England you all take yourselves seriously, all the time. That's what's the matter with England. The trouble with us in Ireland is that we have a sense of humour; now and again we see how ridiculous we are and we go and make fools of ourselves in shame of ourselves. Pretty sound and intricate reasoning that apropos of nothing. (18 March 1924)

The young bloods here rather liked *Thy Neighbour's Wife*, the followers of James Joyce, but they are a very small clique and they have no power. The power among the literary people is wielded by AE and Lennox Robinson and they have the Government behind them. I have won AE over to my side but when he finds out what a scoundrel I have been he will dump me I believe. In about another month however I will have formed a powerful clique of my own and I am going to lick the bunch of them. O'Sullivan of the *Dublin Magazine* likes my writing and accepted three stories from me, one of them "Going Into Exile," but he is an enemy of AE's political views so he is cold except on the matter of accepting good stories for a bad magazine. I have secured the Jewish proprietor of the Irish Book Shop, a good man. And I have secured the wife of Professor Curtiss—which of course is the most important conquest. Now you see that I don't make as many enemies here as I did in London. I have avoided all the Yeats's and the Stevens's etc. They are no good atall.

The Love-Hate Relationship with Story Writing

I received your letter yesterday. Thanks very much for appreciation of "The Blackbird." I felt that it was right and I am very glad that you think it is also. But somehow I get no pleasure from writing those short sketches now. They seem to advance according to a formula and it's like doing a day's work that you have been doing for a long time every day. The uncertainty of achieving anything alone makes literature pleasurable. . . . I am finishing my first Dublin story and I will send it to you on Monday. Local copy.

I am trying to get some place where I can be comfortable and work during the summer but I cannot . . . so far. Dublin is a horrid place for diggings, but it's a great place for doing work. Here I can do three thousand words a day. And I am getting fat. But I better not crow until you tell me whether the words are good or bad. (30 March 1924)

Short stories have lost all interest for me. I brought back several with me but they don't interest me and I don't want to write them. Big ideas devour little ones. Like dominant men, while big ideas are awake and casting about them the little ideas have got to hide or just bow their heads and say "Yes Sir." (27 April 1924)

I am able to do nothing but a weekly sketch for the W.W. [*Weekly Westminster*]. I am writing *piffle* for them as I think they would appreciate it more than literature. If I could only get another little job like that I would be safe—that is unless I break down altogether this time, but I think I will pull around the corner when I get to Ireland. Neurasthenia is a curiously "lively" disease. (16 December 1924)

You will be pleased to hear I wrote another good sketch called "Birth." It's the birth of a calf. Topsy and I claim that it's as good as "The Cow's Death." This is an idyll though. Perhaps it lacks the power of tragedy. I am eagerly looking forward to the drunken pleasure of writing more sketches when I finish my novel. (21 July 1926)

Seán O'Casey's Memory and Critique of O'Flaherty

Some in Dublin hated Yeats, official Catholics feared him, and a group of younger writers disliked his booming opinions on literature and insubstantial things without any local habitation or name. A number of these last, headed by F.R. Higgins, the poet, Liam O'Flaherty and Brinsley Macnamara, the novelists, and Cecil Salkeld, the young painter, had started a Radical Club to nourish the thoughts and ambitions of the young writers, in opposition to the elderly and wild speculation of Yeats and the adulatory group that trailed longingly after him. Some of these wanted to hook in Sean [O'Casey, the author himself] so that his newer influence might be useful in putting Yeats in his improper place. As a preliminary, O'Flaherty brought Edward Garnett to the tenement where he lived, and coaxed Sean to tell Garnett a good deal about the play he was then trying to write, for foolish, innocent Sean had told O'Flaherty something about it. Garnett said he was delighted with the description given, and O'Flaherty bravely simulated the happiness of his companion. On the strength of this praise, O'Flaherty built a hope that Sean would do anything he wished; and so for long, and continuously, he argued against the influence of Yeats on literary thought in Ireland and elsewhere, saying Yeats was too damned arrogant, too assured of the superiority of his own work over that of all the others. Sean, however, had no bubbling desire to be O'Flaherty's gillie, so he countered the arguments used, for he saw clear enough that O'Flaherty, in the way of arrogance and sense of being a superior being, was worse than Yeats, without the elder man's grace and goodwill; while the cloak worn by the storyteller wasn't near so fine or colourful as the fine, silken mantle of poetry draping the shoulders of the poet. . . .

Reprinted from *Inishfallen, Fare Thee Well: Autobiography*. Book 4, 1917–1926 (1949; rpt., London: Pan, 1972), 127, 181.

Sean's plays were stoned with many criticisms from the intellectuals, so that he passed from one bewilderment to another. . . . O'Flaherty's direct announcement (as pompous as anything Yeats could have said) [was] that *"The Plough and the Stars" was a bad play.*

O'Casey's *The Plough and the Stars:*
An Anti-Irish Play

Permit me to protest in your columns against Mr. Yeats' demonstration in the Abbey Theatre on Thursday last. The protest by those who objected to the play (*The Plough and the Stars*) was undoubtedly in bad taste, but nobody loses anything by it, least of all the author, who gained a good advertisement. But the protest by Mr. Yeats, against the protest of the audience, was an insult to the people of this country. I feel that I am personally justified in protesting against his protest because the manner in which they have received my own work (and in all probability the manner in which they WILL receive my work) defends me from the accusation of appealing to the gallery. Allow me to review the position.

In my opinion *The Plough and the Stars* is a bad play. It would be quite in order for an audience to hiss it as a bad play. It was, however, a boorish thing to hiss it because the opinions expressed by the author injured the feelings of the audience. Every man has a right to his opinions. Mr. O'Casey has a right to his opinions. He has a perfect right to protest himself against this treatment of his work by the audience. But Mr. Yeats had positively no right to strut forward and cry with joy that the people of this country had "been cut to the bone." Our people have their faults. It is a good thing that artists should point out these faults. But it is not a good thing that pompous fools should boast that we have been "cut to the bone."

I say WE, because I too was cut to the bone. I am not a Nationalist in the political sense. But I am an admirer of any man who has the courage to die for an ideal. And I think the most glorious gesture in the history of our country was the gesture of those who died in 1916. No great artist in any country in the world refused to give credit, to glorify men who died likewise. Even Tolstoy, the great pacifist, bowed down before the courage of the Cossacks and of their brigand enemies

Reprinted from the *Irish Statesman* 5 (20 February 1926): 739–40.

(even brigands) who died with their death-song on their lips. I bow down before the courage of Pearse and Connolly and their comrades. I did not have the honour to fight with them. But I "am cut to the bone" because an Irish writer did not, unfortunately, do them justice. I do not blame O'Casey. I believe him to be a sincere man. But I am sorry to see him defended by a man who stirred this country to foment enthusiasm for idealism in the last generation. . . .

Sir, I am of Gaelic stock. My ancestors came into this country sword in hand, as conquerors, as the Danes came and the Normans and the English. To conquer is the right of the strong. We who conquered once have been in turn conquered. I acclaim our conquerors. But now the conquered and the conquerors are one. And out of their seed another race has sprung. We are all brothers. All but those who turn their backs on their people and cry, spitting, that they "have been cut to the bone." It was not so that McCracken cried, or Tone, or Emmet, or even the great Parnell.

Finally, I do not believe in political nationalism. I do not believe in Empires. . . .

I believe in the political union of the human race, in the ideal of human brotherhood. But there always will be strife and struggle. Soon perhaps that strife will be intellectual competition. But it is certain that always people born in one place will love that place and try to make it pre-eminent by the achievements of its people. And always brave men will love the weak and struggle with them. And always poets will side with the weak against the strong, and not with the strong against the weak and ignorant. And always great men will not become embittered, even as Synge did not become embittered, but smiled gently like a Christ at those who reviled him.

Passion as Genius

A work of genius . . . must offer something more than a perfect style, the imprint of a cultured mind and . . . gentleness of soul. . . . It must be a relentless picture of life, as lashing in its cruelty as the whip of Christ when there are moneychangers to be beaten from the Temple, as remorseless as the questions of a jealous lover. It must have the power to invoke great beauty or great horror in the same breath as it calls forth laughter from the lips.

Reprinted from "Mr. Tasker's Gods," *Irish Statesman* 3 (7 March 1925): 827.

"Great God of Passion"

It is in these two forms that all poetry has been composed, lyric beauty and epic power. Which is the greater? To me the battle and the blood, the terrible Genghiz, with his camel herds, his hosts of horsemen and his jewelled concubines, the storming of Troy, the war for the great bull of Cuailgne, all the terrible madnesses of men and women crashing their bodies and their minds against the boundary walls of human knowledge. . . .

Great God of Passion, whose hoary face is inscribed with the lines of greatest poetry that man has written and in whose fruitful loins still rest Iliads of verse and prose, to be written on the still unconquered stars, in commemoration of the rout of Jahveh and his angels, by man the unappeaseable conqueror, let you act as judge.

Reprinted from *Joseph Conrad: An Appreciation* (London: E. Lahr, 1930), 7–8, 11.

Energy and Tumult as Cultural Progress

In Ireland, to my mind, we have reached the point in the progress of our race, the point which marked the appearance of Shakespeare in English literature. Let us not be ashamed that gunshots are heard in our streets. Let us rather be glad. For force is, after all, the opposite of sluggishness. . . .

Ours is the wild tumult of the unchained storm, the tumult of the army on the march, clashing its cymbals, rioting with excess of energy. Need we be ashamed of it?

Reprinted from "National Energy," *Irish Statesman* 3 (18 October 1924): 171.

The Need for Indigenous
Irish Culture

We must begin at home. In art, in literature, in architecture, in general culture, we are submerged beneath the rotting mound of British traditions, traditions which have their spiders' legs in the columns of the *Irish Statesman* as securely as they have them in the illiterate columns of the Irish Republican organ from Suffolk St.

From "A View of Irish Culture," *Irish Statesman* 4 (20 June 1925): 461.

Shadow-Boxing with
Narrative Voice

When His Excellency the Governor-General heard that I was about to write his life, he humorously threatened to write my life in revenge. I had to hurry with my life of him, in order to reach the public with my account of his life, before he reached the public with his account of my life. My haste was largely influenced by the knowledge, as he himself stated at a public dinner, that my life written by him would be much more interesting than his life written by me. So that the clumsiness and mediocrity of my effort would have a better chance of evading comparison with a subtle and elegant work, by appearing in print while His Excellency was still writing an account of my miserable career.

I must also admit that His Excellency's humorous threat has greatly influenced the style, method and temper of my trifling life of him. Because, I realized that if I were to escape with my life from the critics, who would be sure to compare the two lives, I must as closely as possible copy the methods in which His Excellency's life of me would be sure to be written. In order to do this, I had to make a radical change in my previous methods of writing. I had to approach my material with a certain childish abandonment, respect nothing and irritate wherever possible. I have done so. And now that I have finished the business, I am a trifle awed by the result. For I hardly recognize it as my own work. It seems that I have been possessed while writing it by some merry imp; no, not always merry, but devilishly bitter at times. I have read it over. It is the most inconsistent book I ever read. The man who wrote it, or rather the spirit that wrote it, must be as changeable as a weathercock in an uncertain wind. I myself am an artist, without any definite convictions about human affairs, other than those subtle aspects of life which are of interest to an artist. But the individual who wrote this is an extremely prejudiced fellow, almost a Jesuit. I know nothing about politics and care less. But the author of this work sets out to tell the whole human race how the business of politics must be

Reprinted from *The Life of Tim Healy* (London: Jonathan Cape, 1927), 5–6.

conducted with benefit to the entire world. His conclusions seem to me appalling. All classes of human beings are of equal interest to me as an artist, but here I find an odious discrimination made as between various classes. As an artist I believe that standards of justice, of right and wrong, of good and evil, merely serve as social scales, in which goods for sale are judged; constantly changing with the nature and condition of the articles offered for sale and the conditions under which they are purchased. But the author of this book very impudently measures every human act as if he carried about him, on his person, a large series of gods and all of them infallible.

I say, dear readers, in abject self-defence, that every word in this book must be taken with a grain of salt. Let the whole book be read from the point of view of the merry and sometimes malicious imp that wrote it. I declare by my father's honour that that imp is no relative of mine. I entirely disown him and having finished this work, I am glad to say that I have reverted to my former nature, of a modest artist, who mutely bows his head before the stones hurled at him by his loving fellow-countrymen.

Censorship in Ireland

During the Eucharistic Congress recently held in Dublin, I was staying in a small Kerry town. It has a population of two thousand people and fifty-three public houses. Like almost every other Irish provincial town, it is incredibly dirty and sordid to look upon. In the long back street inhabited by the proletariat I came across human excrement at every second step. There was no vestige of culture in the place. The three local priests were sour and secretive fellows, who confined their activities to the prevention of fornication, dancing and reading. The only pastime permitted to the males was drinking in the fifty-three public houses. The females wandered about with a hungry expression in their eyes. Shortly after my arrival, the priests of the diocese held a mass dinner at my hotel, to devise ways and means for getting me out of the county, as a menace to faith and morals; but without any success.

Then the Eucharistic Congress came along and the populace, exalted by some extraordinary fanaticism, decorated the town with bunting. In the proletarian slum, several altars were erected in the open air. Around these altars some people recited the rosary at night, while others played accordions, danced and drank stout.

However no attempt was made to remove the dung from the streets, nor any fraction of the dirt which desecrated the walls of the houses and the floors of the taverns. I walked up and down the town, pointing from the bunting to the pavement and saying: "Bunting, dung. Dung, bunting." It was considered sacrilegious.

Unclean offal of any sort, whether in my neighborhood or in the minds of people with whom I have association, is strongly distasteful to me. So is poverty, ungracious tyranny and ignoble suffering. In my work I have been forced in honesty to hold up a mirror to life as I found it in my country. And, of necessity, the mirror shows the dung about the pretty altars. So a censorship has been imposed upon my work, since it is considered sacrilegious by the Irish Church that I should object to the sordid filth around the altars.

Reprinted from "The Irish Censorship," *American Spectator* 1 (November 1932): 2.

Part 2

The tyranny of the Irish Church and its associate parasites, the up-start Irish bourgeoisie, the last posthumous child from the wrinkled womb of European capitalism, maintains itself by the culture of dung, superstition and ignoble poverty among the masses. And the censorship of literature was imposed, lest men like me could teach the Irish masses that contact with dung is demoralizing, that ignorance is ignoble and that poverty, instead of being a passport to Heaven, makes this pretty earth a monotonous Hell. The soutaned bullies of the Lord, fortressed in their dung-encrusted towns, hurl the accusation of sexual indecency at any book that might plant the desire for civilization and freedom in the breasts of their wretched victims.

So they have set up a censorship of books in Ireland, and now at Irish ports, whose sole export is porter and men of genius, imported literature which is the product of Irish genius is seized and burned as dangerous contraband. And so tortured Ireland, which a few years ago asked for and received the sympathy of the world's intellectuals, now shows herself as a surly, sick bitch biting the hand that fed her.

But it's not true of Ireland, nor of the mass of Irishmen and Irishwomen. Slaves cannot be blamed for the vices of their masters. I am censored and abhorred by the illiterate ruffians who control Irish life at present. There is hardly a single newspaper in Ireland that would dare print anything I write. There is hardly a bookshop in Ireland that would dare show my books in its windows. There is hardly a library that would not be suppressed for having my books on its shelves. Outside Dublin not a single organization would dare ask me to address them. Yet I claim that Ireland is the only country where I feel of any consequence as a writer. It is the only country where I feel the youth and freshness of Spring among the people, where I feel at one with my mates, where I sing with their singing and weep with their weeping, where I feel that I am a good workman doing a useful job and honored for my craft.

Ireland is no land of barbarians and there are no people in the world who love art and beauty more than the Irish. But alas! Our little island has been stricken with a triple mange of friars, gombeen men and poverty. The soutaned witch-doctors have spread terror among our simple folk and, as one goes through the country, it is pathetic to meet in every little town and village timid, whispering individuals who say, "It's terrible here. I can't get anything to read on account of the priests. Have you got any of your books you could lend me?" In the same way, I was told by an eminent London publisher that he receives bundles of letters from sexually-starved Irishwomen, asking for bawdy books. Book-

118

legging may soon become on a small scale quite as profitable as the prohibition of alcohol made bootlegging in America.

Bawdy books! Bawdy houses! Booze! On these three forms of vulgar entertainment there seemed to be no censorship whatsoever during the Eucharistic Congress in Dublin. The town was wide open all night and every night. Then the mob went back home to purify themselves by scratching their backs against hair shirts. The militant puritans in Ireland have, in my opinion, staged their last great parade. Before very long they'll be all hurled into the clean Atlantic, together with their censorship, their dung, their bawdy books, their bawdy houses and their black booze. Then we can once more in Ireland have wine and love and poetry; become a people famed, as of old, "for beauty and amorousness."

The Ironies of the
Irish Language Fanatics

To the Editor of the *Irish Statesman*.
Dear Sir,—Una McC. Dix, whoever she is, is a very foolish person. Otherwise she would not draw my attention to her existence in the manner she has done in your current issue. Because now, as the Governor-General said, I am going to find out all about her and for the same reason as His Excellency.

Apart from that, in order to prevent more gadflies from worrying this labouring horse (I am quoting Tchehov), I am going to tell the lady why I don't write in Irish. Even though her name is Dix and therefore more likely to be interested in my reasons for not writing in the language of her ancestors.

I have written in Irish. I wrote in Irish when I was sixteen. I won a gold medal from an organisation in Philadelphia for some Irish prose at that age, and procured a holiday, as far as I can remember, for the whole of Rockwell as a result. Yes, and a leading article from the *Tipperary Nationalist*. That was a few years before the great war. I wonder was Una McC. Dix at that time interested in the Irish language?

When I began to write professionally I was no longer interested in the Irish language from a political point of view. I was more interested in politics and in the Irish people. I felt, in my young arrogance, that some ideas which I had picked up around the world might be useful to the Irish people, and I chose the best language for presenting these ideas to my people. As the people spoke English I naturally wrote in English. If I wrote in Irish they would not be able to read the stuff. And, of course, as the editor kindly remarked, no printer in Ireland would print the stuff, either in Irish or in English.

Two years later I became less interested in politics and in the regeneration of the Irish people, intellectually; having come to the conclusion that my people were too hopelessly sunk in intellectual barbarism

Reprinted from "Writing in Gaelic," *Irish Statesman* 9 (17 December 1927): 348.

to be capable of being saved by a single man. The Shannon Scheme appeared to me to be more capable of doing the job. So I was seized, like George Moore, with a sudden desire to use the Irish language as a medium of expression. I wrote a few short stories for the Gaelic League organ. They printed them and sent me three copies of the issue in which they were printed. Then I consulted Padraig O Conaire and we decided that drama was the best means of starting a new literature in Irish. I became fearfully enthusiastic. The two of us went to Dublin and entered a hall where some fellows were holding a Gaeltacht Commission. We put our scheme before them for a travelling theatre and so on. I guaranteed to write ten plays. They thought we were mad and, indeed, took very little interest in us. In fact, I could see by their looks and their conversation that they considered us immoral persons.

However, I was undaunted. I wrote a play and gave it to Gearoid O Lochlainn. He liked it and got the Gaelic Drama League to produce it. That was not easy. Because some horrifying Christians from the Education Department threatened fire and brimstone if they staged my work, on the ground that I was an immoral person. In fact, I believe, they had to pack the hall with detectives in order to prevent the Gaelic Christians from throwing my unfortunate play to the lions.

Although the theatre was packed, which rarely happens for these Gaelic plays, I was never paid for the production.

Here is the joke. The only remuneration I received for this play was from an English Socialist who dislikes Irish and everything connected with nationalism of any sort in any place. He paid me twenty five pounds for the Gaelic manuscript, i.e., for my handwriting.

I naturally swore that I would never write another word in Irish. If I do write in Irish I'll take good care not to publish it and place it at the mercy of these sows.

I don't write for money. If I wanted to write for money I could be a rich man now. I am a good craftsman and I am cunning enough to understand the various follies of mankind and womankind. In fact, if I ever get so hard up that I'll lose my self respect, I'll start a religious paper in the Irish language and make a fortune on it.

I write to please myself and two friends. One is my wife and the other is Mr. Edward Garnett. I don't write for Una McC Dix, and for that reason I'd be pleased if she refrained from drawing my attention to her existence. Because I just love writing about gadflies.

Liam O'Flaherty

P.S.—In answer to Messrs. Chambers and Colum, permit me to say

Interview, 1946: "Irish Revival Delights Liam O'Flaherty"

"In recent years I heard much about a scarcity of writers in Irish. The first day I was back in Dublin convinced me that this is a fallacy," Liam O'Flaherty, the writer, told an *Irish Press* reporter on Saturday.

Mr. O'Flaherty went to the United States before the war, was "marooned" for six years and landed in Cobh last week. He picked up his daughter, Pegeen, who lives in West Cork, and they came to Dublin on Thursday.

"One of the first things I did here was to tour the Gum [*an Gúm* ("the Plan"), the Irish government's publisher] and the bookshops. . . . I renewed acquaintance with books by the older hands like MacGrianna.

. . . There were fine stories by Tomás Bairead."

"Then I came across a charming book about wanderings in Mayo. I forget the name and the name of the author, but in the middle of it I found an old song that I sang in Aran as a child and it brought back many memories." Here O'Flaherty burst into the old sean-nos song in his soft, warm, Galway voice very slightly tinged by an American drawl.

From this point he went on to speak animatedly about the Gaelic revival.

"There has been a great change," he declared. "Meet somebody in the streets of Dublin and start talking to him in Irish. He will reply in the language."

. . . While in America he wrote a number of short stories in Irish, and he is hoping to have those published here soon.

He is enthusiastic about the idea of a Gaelic theatre. He recalled that himself and Pádraic Ó Conaire once set out to establish a touring Gaelic theatre. O'Flaherty wrote a play for it, "Dorchadas" (Darkness), but the theatre was never born. "At the time there was too much narrow prejudice against it," he said, "and also we had the very patriotic Cosgrave government."

In the United States O'Flaherty lived most of the time in a lonely house in the middle of a wood in Connecticut, and wrote in Irish and English. He came out from his retreat to speak for Irish neutrality at meetings sponsored by the Irish-American Neutrality League.

"That small voice," he said, "was one of the meagre weapons used against the barrage of propaganda against Ireland during the war.

"The Americans fell for the propaganda, and as an Irishman and an advocate of neutrality I found myself very unpopular in the cities. So I retired to the woods."

Propaganda Nourished

Mr. O'Flaherty said that the anti-Irish prejudice was nourished solely by propaganda, and when the propaganda receded after the war it disappeared. After the war there was a period of disillusion, and people began to ask if, after all, there could be a case for neutrality.

He said Mr. de Valera's handling of the Churchill situation made a tremendous impression in the U.S. "It was superb statesmanship."

I asked him, What do you think of the new Ireland in relation to the things you wrote so bitterly about in the twenties?

He said Ireland seemed to be forging ahead to prosperity and to proper social conditions. The people seemed to have got self-reliance and determination to work for their country.

I suppose there is no need to ask you what you think about censorship? I asked.

He replied—"Strangely enough, I agree with censorship, but not as it is worked here. Ban books in bad taste; ban the filthy and the vulgar, but be very careful not to ban literature. With all this Sexton Blake and other stuff, we cannot train our people to a proper appreciation of real literature.

Film Scripts in Irish

He has strong views about the film. He would ban the mass of what he calls Hollywood trash and would sponsor cultural films.

He spoke very enthusiastically about an Irish film industry. He said that we have the creative and mechanical genius for it. He would confine the scripts to Irish and see that the films were really cultural.

There would be a tremendous demand for them in the United States and other countries, with English sub-titles, and simultaneously we would be moulding our own taste, he said. In New York at the moment a French film, with English sub-titles, was running for seven months; another was also running a long time; both are good for at least two years, he added.

He has written a book on the Land League, *Land*. It has just been published in the U.S. and will be published in England by Gollancz. He says it is more virile than *Famine* and has more exciting situations.

He was very hesitant when I asked him what he considered his best book. He was silent for a moment and then said laughingly: "I am always finding fault with them. I do not think any of them is good."

Energetic as Ever

Mr. O'Flaherty is very bronzed; his powerful body is as energetic as ever and he looks quite boyish. Before talking he insisted on seeing that I was comfortable; then he burst into a torrent of words, gesticulating excitedly, and moved from chair to chair, his big sea-blue eyes flashing and the dimples sinking into his cheeks.

He had not had time to renew old acquaintances, but he asked after many old friends. He was met here by Peadar O'Donnell.

Soon he will go back to his old home in Aran, where he will meet relatives and Pat Mullen and Dr. O'Brien. He will be here for some time. Whether he will afterwards take up the threads of world wanderings is not known—whether people will again be asking, "Where is Liam O'Flaherty now?"

THE CRITICS

Introduction

This final section is a kind of "greatest hits" of O'Flaherty criticism from the earliest reviews of his work (beginning in 1924) through recent scholarship (stopping in 1988). Among other selections, this section excerpts the work of the authors of three books about O'Flaherty (John Zneimer, Paul Doyle, and Angeline Kelly). Each of these books (as well as the books by James H. O'Brien and Patrick Sheeran) is readily available in good libraries, so I've chosen only a few short quotations that exemplify particular critical themes. I recommend that the reader consult these books, particularly Angeline Kelly's, the only previous book specifically on O'Flaherty's short fiction.

O'Flaherty has attracted, at the same time, his share of negative criticism (for example, John Crawford's review, quoted at the beginning of my chapter on satire and comedy). I do not include any of that here, as my limited space is best devoted to important, thoughtful criticism in periodicals, collected and made easily accessible for readers who would otherwise have to struggle to obtain it. Reprinted first are several observant early comments from reviewers—Richard Church (1924), an anonymous essayist in the *Irish Statesman* (1927), and William Troy (1930). One of the earliest critical predictions was offered in May 1924 by Æ (George Russell) in his *Irish Statesman*: "The future development of Liam O'Flaherty will be watched with intense interest by many. Can he write out of more than one mood? If he can . . . his name may be very great in Irish literature."[1] Troy's assessment, the earliest attempt at a systematic overview, can be taken as the real beginning of O'Flaherty scholarship. The passage from Rhys Davies's 1932 preface is insightful, as are Seán Ó Faoláin's review of O'Flaherty's major 1937 collection of stories and Frank O'Connor's review of the 1956 collection. Here we have O'Flaherty's two most accomplished immediate Irish contemporaries and fellow masters of the short story reviewing his two best known anthologies.

O'Flaherty criticism entered a new phase with H. E. Bates's evaluation of his work in *The Modern Short Story* (1941) and George Brandon

Saul's 1956 article "A Wild Sowing: The Short Stories of Liam O'Flaherty." Saul was the first scholar in a position to take a fairly comprehensive look at the short fiction, since most of it had been published by 1956. His is a useful and balanced critique, though he does seem a rather stodgy New Critic in a couple of his complaints.

O'Flaherty attracted considerable scholarly interest during the 1970s (when all of the five earlier books on his work appeared). In the brief passage quoted here, Paul Doyle astutely considers style, tone, and satire in the stories. Contemporary critical emphases became evident during the 1970s: John Zneimer decided that O'Flaherty was an existentialist; Helene O'Connor, an ecologist; George O'Brien, a modernist. Of course, part of O'Flaherty's chameleon fascination was that he was capable of being each of these.

Vivian Mercier was the first to ask the still not completely answered question of why O'Flaherty essentially stopped writing after the early 1950s. In another article Mercier argued that O'Flaherty wrote for the eye rather than the ear, but the impact of his stories on the ear as well was illustrated by Angeline Kelly (who examined both "Visual and Aural Effects" in his stories) and Brendan Kennelly (who demonstrated that "Wild Stallions" "falls naturally into verse").

Last but not least, and as in the case of part 2, this section concludes with excerpts about the relationship of O'Flaherty's short fiction to the Irish language and bilingualism. The fact that the five writers who treat this subject range from Tomás de Bhaldraithe in 1968 to William Daniels in 1988 suggests that this may remain one of the richest areas of research. Broderick and Eoghan Ó hAnluain both attest to the large positive influence of O'Flaherty's stories on writers such as themselves and the Irish reading public. The seminal study of his bilingualism was Tomás de Bhaldraithe's "Liam O'Flaherty—Translator (?)" (1968). Maureen Murphy (1973) and William Daniels (1988) are two American scholars who have followed up de Bhaldraithe's work in this area. The selection from Daniels's article is an appropriate one with which to conclude part 3, as it comprises a review of criticism on the subject.

Note

1. Æ (George Russell), review of *The Black Soul*, *The Irish Statesman* 2 (3 May 1924): 244.

Richard Church

Liam O'Flaherty is a name that first attracted me some time ago as the subscription to a vivid and heartbreaking short story called "The Cow's Death," which appeared in the *New Statesman*. It was altogether different from the literary and artful short story which is characteristic of our English dealings with this difficult form. Yet it was not the product of a rustic genius that had only to come to town to be swamped and spoiled. It was absolutely mature, with a terseness and cleanness of expression that could be obtained only by the expense of much wealth of concealment. Surely, I felt, if ever work was produced by conscientious care, this author has that power of passionate conscience in abundance. I felt that in these thousand or so words the effort of an intense emotion, expressed fully yet economically, could be the result only of religious zeal. Now that I have read this collection of stories, which contains "The Cow's Death," I am more than ever convinced that the author is a zealot for perfect expression. What he has achieved in this book is remarkable, and I do not hesitate favourably to compare his work with that of the most expert writers of the short story, such established names as Ambrose Bierce, Stephen Crane, Katherine Mansfield, Mr. Wells, and Mr. Hardy. Following Synge in modern Irish literature, he should, with Mr. Joyce, give the quietus to the Celtic Twilight movement, whose lovely evening has been followed by such a depressing night.

He confines himself for subject-matter entirely to Irish life among the peasants, the animals, the fish, and the elements of earth, air and water. Even when writing of these last terrestrial powers he confines them, by the force of his native genius, to the locality of Irish villages and shores. But that confinement serves to accelerate their speed and earth-consuming rage, and they battle under this restriction all the more convincingly. . . .

Reprinted from "A Holiday Task," *Spectator Literary Supplement* (4 October 1924): 468.

There is no doubt that his realistic method owes much to the French masters in this kind, to whom he may have come through the George Moore of *Esther Waters* and *The Mummer's Wife*. But there is more of the sympathizer about him than there is in these masters, in whom the observer predominates. He has, therefore, much of Tchekov. But above all, I feel that he has a distinct quality in common with his own countryman, Oliver Goldsmith, whose lovable and inspired personality recurred again and again to me while I was reading these stories.

There are indications here and there in the book that the author is not yet out of his apprenticeship. I am not quite convinced that his self-expression is to be through his realistic method, especially if he forces it too far towards its French and American sources. I receive at present the impression that he is disciplining himself mercilessly, excising his own temperament to the point of self-discouragement. There is a phrase recurring frequently in the book which betrays him. After some meticulous description, he will round it all off with a weary gesture by the phrase "or something," as though he is chafing against his self-imposed task. There are, too, patches of misplaced detailed description, as when he points out minutiae of dress *after* he has set his characters in action. This holds up his movement, and gives his fine terse writing a tinge of short-winded garrulity. To put aside my quibblings, I can only pay my homage to his sanity, his profound love and pity for mortal, beast, stones, trees, and all things static and moving, that makes the setting for, and furnish the actors in this coastal and rustic life of Ireland.

"Y. O." (Anonymous)

Twenty-five years ago Anglo-Irish literature was romantic, idealist or mystic. But what change in the writers who came after these. . . .

In what a remote world are O'Grady's *Bardic History* and *Flight of the Eagle* if we set them beside *The Informer* or *Mr. Gilhooley* by Liam

Reprinted from "Literature and Life: Heredity in Literature," *Irish Statesman* 8 (4 June 1927): 304.

O'Flaherty. What has happened in the national being that a quarter of a century should have brought about such a change? From the most idealistic literature in Europe we have reacted so that with Joyce, O'Flaherty and O'Casey, the notabilities of the movement, we have explored the slums of our cities, the slums of the soul. Is there a law in these oscillations like that which brings centrifugal to balance centripetal? Are these writers the black spots which balance the bright stars? If a writer of powerful characters appears is it inevitable that his opposite must be born? . . .

Standish O'Grady would disown the child whose literary existence I surmise his Cuchulain Saga made inevitable. That O'Grady's *Cuchulain*, that fusion of fire and gentleness, the inevitably heroic, should have for offspring the *Informer* will call forth endless repudiations. But the law demands it and logic accepts it for all the irony of the situation so created. If *Cuchulain* had not been so noble the *Informer* would not have been so ignoble. If O'Grady had written stories with characters like Jane Austen's, does anybody believe that the *Informer* would have been necessitated as the logical reaction? As is the case with Yeats and Joyce, where the literary heredity is seen in the fact that both are stylists, so in the case of O'Grady and O'Flaherty, the character is common and the tendency in both is to action. . . .

The moment we read a book either of two things take place. We find the book is akin to us and we accept it, or if it is not ours we react from it and tend to give birth in ourselves to the opposite idea. If we cannot accept ideal characters like O'Grady we are turned to the work which has the reality of life to us. If we hate the Informers or Blooms or Gilhooleys we inevitably will seek out the idealists.

William Troy

Liam O'Flaherty, at the age of thirty-two, has written five novels, four volumes of short stories, a biography and a large number of sketches and short stories soon to be gathered together in another collection.

Reprinted from "The Position of Liam O'Flaherty," *Bookman* 72 (November 1930): 7, 10, 11.

His reputation, however, is commensurate neither with this record of sustained creative energy nor with the easily recognizable distinction of his work. Literary popularity is never a matter of significance in speaking about a serious artist; but the reasons behind the critical apathy in the present instance are more interesting than usual. To consider them is to discover something about the mechanism of literary popularity at any time. It is also one excellent means of approaching certain of the essential features of this writer's contribution to the literature of our age. For the two things which are responsible for the neglect of O'Flaherty are at the same time inseparable from the deepest meaning and value of his work: his nationality and his fondness for melodrama.

The disadvantages of being an Irish writer today would be numerous even were it possible for the English reviews to be less loyal to their country and their class. Liam O'Flaherty has had at least as much to overcome in detaching himself from the settled mist of the "Celtic renaissance" as the writers of that movement had in detaching themselves from the earlier schools of Lever and Boucicault. The unfortunate result is that O'Flaherty has perhaps suffered more than he has gained by the association. It would seem pretty definite that the critical portion of the public is as avid of novelty as the common reader: and both certainly have had reason of late to become rather stalely habituated to the periodic emergence of ambitious talent in Ireland. At any rate an unmistakable tone of weariness has become the custom in whatever is written about this writer in the few literary journals which do not altogether ignore him. Actually, O'Flaherty's relation to the double tradition of Anglo-Irish literature is unique and distinct. He is on the side of Synge and Joyce, as against the side of Swift and Shaw; but he does not belong unreservedly with either of those writers. Neither intellectual refinement nor the impedimenta of culture and religion operate to confuse the complete identification with nature which is the predominant feature of his work. He is closer to the unknown writers of the early Gaelic folk literature than to any of his contemporaries. He is less the product of any modern school than of that period when European culture had not yet entirely lost its innocence. . . .

The stories in *Spring Sowing* and *The Tent* should make their appeal even to those readers who are unable to respond to the larger patterns of the novels. The trained intensity of style, the economy of detail, the exact sharpness of perception appear here with special appropriateness and combine to place these stories among the most distinguished of our time. Almost every phase of Irish life is touched on, although for the most part they deal with the land. Such stories as "Milking Time," "Three Lambs" and the title-story of "Spring Sowing" are themselves like the rich exhalations of the soil: "Going into Exile" is a record of its tragedy, "The Bladder" and "The Old Hunter" of its robust humors. Perhaps the most perfect in achievement of all these little stories is "Birth" (published in the limited edition entitled *The Fairy Goose*), which is the simple account of a group of peasants gathered together near a meadow at night to attend the birth of a calf. But the most individual are those in which O'Flaherty writes about a lost thrush, or the capture of a fish, or a sea gull's first flight—unsentimental studies of animal life written with a fastidious interest usually reserved for human beings alone. From all of O'Flaherty's stories, however, one takes away a similar impression of the profound solidarity of nature, all of her manifestations being of equal importance to the artist who admits her superiority . . . .

. . . Nature, not as the dark intoxicant of the earlier romanticists, but as something apprehended in the flesh, may come to be more and more accepted by our writers as the superstructure of our intellectual world crumbles about their feet. In the meantime, when most of our novelists seem to be frantically entrapped among the ruins, the reading of O'Flaherty is like a tonic and a promise.

Rhys Davies

One notices that immediately his characters enter a city or become town-dwellers a wearisome binge with all its attendant flourishes ensues. Cities drive his characters desperate, and though we too are borne along by the wealth of incidents which befall them, upheld, if protestingly, by their energy, with what a sigh of relief we open another book

Reprinted from the foreword to O'Flaherty's *The Wild Swans and Other Stories* (London: Joiner and Steele, 1932), 8–10.

of O'Flaherty and find ourselves back with the peasants among the farms and along that sea-coast where he is most sensitive.

There he is rich and vital. We lose the sense of printed words and smell the keen spray-cool air of wild spaces that open magically before us. We clearly see the anchored curraghs bobbing over the heavy moonlit silence of the sea, and know there is going to be a bit of real drama presently. We are more than in love with Red Barbara. The blackbirds are revealed to us for ever.

We must be grateful to him too that he has never prettified the country. With him we never take a stroll from the library to the village inn and, after buying a round, encourage the rustic company to talk in rich dialect. He doesn't weave eternal daisy-chains in a meadow that is also delicious with buttercups, sentimentally aware—in a careful style—how tranquil and beautiful is nature. His sheep and goats and cows are alive, suffering and pitiable in travail, observant and critical in well-being: they *are* sheep and goats, not things about which one can become literary. Neither do we have the feeling that his pieces of scenery have been let down from above or wheeled in from the wings, as one does in the stories of, say, Katherine Mansfield and those that run after her.

But the town is forever Babylon to him. Only disaster can come out of it. He is attuned to the roar of the waves, the sweep of the winds in remote villages, the pointed and humorous chattering of peasant voices (when they speak to each other and not to visitors). He has the kind of subtlety and wit that does not depend on sophistication and elegance. He is not profound except in the sense that man's conflict with elemental things is profound. He has no philosophy except that of a simple man's enjoyment of what comes to his hand: a good drink, a Red Barbara of a woman, a pot of money. His books do not shatter us with their spiritual experiences or move us to fury at the baseness of civilization. But he tells a tale of a wild swan startled into flight from death, or a miser who swallows his money as he lies dying, or a sturdy young man who takes to his bed because of the howling sickness that has come with love, and his exhibitions of life's primal forces, though they may lack the development of sophisticated passion, become memorable in their simple directness.

And perhaps, even in these days of Proust and Joyce and Mrs. Woolf, his way is the more eternal.

Seán Ó Faoláin

I have spoken of O'Flaherty as being at the head of the realistic school of his day; it is realism with a difference, and strangely, he is far and away at his best when, in his short stories, he is not writing in that tradition at all. . . . Essentially, I do believe, O'Flaherty is, like every known Irish writer, an inverted romantic. If he were a true realist he would look at life, and whatever faults he found with it, he would write of it with gusto. But there is in O'Flaherty less gusto than disgust. If he were a true romantic he would not see reality at all, he would see only his dreams. But, as I have said, he is no fool, and when he has sought out, in his adventurous way, some fresh world, some hoped-for ideal, some smiling Dulcinea, he sees the old familiar pimply face of the priest's niece behind the powder and paint. Neither a realist, nor a romantic, then, nor yet a naturalistic writer, he sets out in the most self-conscious and deliberate way to attack with violence the things that hurt the inarticulated dream of his romantic soul. For he *has* a romantic soul; he has the inflated ego of the romantic, the dissatisfaction of the romantic, the grand imagination, the response to the magic of nature, the self-pity of the romantic, his masochistic rage, the unbalance. And these are the claws in which he takes reality and, like a gull with a shellfish, he lifts it up to an enormous height and lets it fall with a crash; while we are yet stunned by his gyring flight, and the reverberation of the impact, he then swoops to see if there is anything worth his respect in what he has already destroyed and, screaming, he flies away, unsatisfied.

In those lovely short stories, however, he is at rest. There he has found something that bears a resemblance to his ideal. Not in men, but in birds and animals; and often men are seen as cruel creatures who hunt and torment these dumb things. In *Spring Sowing* there is a perfect, a lovely, a tender story called "Three Lambs," and there, as in those other excellent stories, "The Hook," "The Cow's Death," "The

Reprinted from "Don Quixote O'Flaherty," *London Mercury* 37 (December 1937): 173–74.

137

Rockfish," one has the feeling that O'Flaherty has his ear to the earth, listening quietly.

The best of his short stories have now been opportunely collected into one volume, fifty-eight stories that are the pure distillation of natural genius. It is a bold saying, but I do believe that no book published this winter can come within a donkey's bray of it.

Frank O'Connor

O'Flaherty never forgets that his stories are news. If Moore's "Home Sickness" is one of my few standards of what a great story should be, there are at least three or four of O'Flaherty's which haunt me in the same way. Mr. Mercier's introduction compares O'Flaherty with Synge. I find it difficult to see a single point of comparison. He is on much safer ground when comparing him with D. H. Lawrence. My own tendency being to run hard whenever I see an animal, I can only offer as an act of faith the belief that O'Flaherty's animal stories are masterly presentations of instinctual life, but when he describes the instinctual life of human beings—of children, women and men from his own wild countryside—there is no question in my mind that he writes as a master. He has all Lawrence's power of conveying the enchantment of the senses which is part of the instinctual life and, unlike Lawrence, does not romanticize or rationalize it. He begins to go false only when he has to deal with people who are compelled to live by their judgment rather than their instincts, and this, and not any theological dispute, seems to me the real basis of his quarrel with Catholicism in Ireland.

Whatever O'Flaherty stories may lack, it is not the narrative impulse, because he comes from the Aran Islands, one of the last outposts of folk culture, and his native language is Irish. And since, like a Munsterwoman I once spoke to about him, "I do be lighting candles to Liam O'Flaherty," let me state my only complaints against his work, which are that his English lacks the distinction and beauty of his Gaelic, and his form is occasionally very dull indeed.

Reprinted from "A Good Short Story Must Be News," *New York Times Book Review*, 10 June 1956, 1, 20.

In spite of the powerful narrative line, O'Flaherty's form is an art form, not a folk one; but it is the convenient, ready-to-wear magazine form of the Twenties in England—two to three thousand words describing a single episode—and while, like the ready-to-wear suit it is a great convenience, the pattern is also in quantity very monotonous.

O'Flaherty once said to me, "If you can describe a hen crossing a road you are a real writer," and of course plunged me in gloom for days because I knew if the hen were waiting for me to describe her, she wouldn't even do, boiled, for an Irish hotel on a Sunday afternoon. I finally added the saying to the sayings of other great writers (like Chekhov's "To do a thing with the minimum of movements is the definition of grace") which I found essential to an understanding of their work but of no particular help in improving my own.

Yet, as the work of Tolstoy shows, the instincts account for a great part of human character, and O'Flaherty's range is remarkable. If I had to choose one story of his to stand beside "Home Sickness" as one of the great masterpieces of storytelling, I should, I think, choose "The Fairy Goose." . . . In essence, the story tells the whole history of religion. The absurdity of the cult seems to call for satire, for an Anatole France or a Norman Douglas, but by a miracle of taste and feeling O'Flaherty never permits the shadow of a sneer to disturb the gravity of the theme. We laugh—laugh louder indeed than we would laugh at France or Douglas—but at the same time we are moved, and eventually the impression left on our mind is that of Turgenev's "Byezhin Meadow"—itself one of the great masterpieces of storytelling—of a vast sense of life's mystery and beauty.

H. E. Bates

O'Flaherty, like many another writer just beginning, had cosmopolitan notions of writing, wanted to let off political crackers, and instantly chose to write of the life (*i.e.*, London) he knew least. O'Flaherty, greatly fancying himself as a tough realist, forgot the poet in himself

From *The Modern Short Story: A Critical Survey* (Surrey, England: Thomas Nelson, 1941), 157–59. Reprinted by permission of the Estate of H. E. Bates.

and set out to reproduce the more lurid shades of Maupassant. His work was seen by Edward Garnett, who promptly dispatched O'Flaherty to Ireland, advised him to look at his own people and, in his own words, "write a story about a cow." From that very sensible advice there came a spate of vivid sketches and stories about Irish peasants and fishermen which had the freshness of new paint. From the birth of a lamb, the death of a cow, the first flight of a blackbird, the peasant hatred of brothers, even from the progression of an Atlantic wave gathering and hurling itself against the Aran rocks, O'Flaherty extracted a wild, tender, and sometimes violently nervous beauty. Untamed words were hurled like stabs of paint on the page; the world of sea and craggy fields and animal peasants was seen, like Maupassant's, in a vivid glare of light. Emotions here were primitive: passion, greed, physical violence, jealousy, hatred, love, hunger, poverty. Men and women moved with a raw animal fury and lust that was checked only by the inevitable fear of priestly wrath and the terrors of hell.

That world had much in common with Maupassant's, and O'Flaherty, as a novelist scrappy, sensational, and often cheap, had a keen and relentless eye for its colour, its drama, its contradictory forces of greed and religion, simplicity and craftiness, devotion and deception, and not least its primitively beautiful background of sea, earth, and sky. In consequence his stories give the effect of pictures dynamically conceived and flashed on a screen. The leisurely refined compassion of Joyce is missing; the precious musical periods of Moore are absent. Everything has in it a kind of impatient sting, a direct stabbing physical force, brutal, sensuous, and elemental. . . .

. . . O'Flaherty, like Maupassant, saw life in a strong light, dramatically, powerfully. Energy alone is not enough, but the sensuous poetic energy of O'Flaherty was like a flood; the reader was carried away by it and with it, slightly stunned and exalted by the experience.

George Brandon Saul

Spring Sowing is a markedly lyrical collection; its reflections of Aran are fresh and those of revolutionary Dublin life lively, especially since O'Flaherty has had by choice a vast personal experience of war and revolution. . . . *Spring Sowing* itself tells of a young peasant couple of the island of Inverara during their first spring sowing together: this is an event of both practical and symbolical significance . . . to them though one also prophetic of weary years ahead. Here is the O'Flaherty who is sensitive to the gentleness that can set a glow even on life that is cruelly primitive and poverty-wounded.

These stories certainly are various enough in both subject matter and appeal, and are suggestive of work to follow: a cow, seeing her dead calf in the tides, commits suicide from a cliff; a little boy is exhilarated by a lambing; a peasant sells a pig, gets drunk, and makes a fool of himself; a bullock and a wild sow are cruelly abused; two drunken young men quarrel in a curragh and are drowned; three fishermen land their curragh safely against dangerous odds; a cowardly young sea gull is tricked into flying by his mother; etc. The best tales are generally those which are closest to the soil and also to the beasts and human beings (the implied distinction is not always convincing) most nearly akin to it. Sometimes, however, the author's characteristic "psychological" analyses of the behaviour and assumed mental processes of brute animals are more imaginative than persuasive, however accurate his reports of physical responses, which seem based on sensitive and minute observation. A blackbird, for instance, is pictured as singing with self-conscious vanity and is ascribed motivations of a human sort. And of course there is O'Flaherty's interest—a recurrent concern—in detailed descriptions of sadistic, and sometimes nauseating, brutality: hence "Sport: The Kill" and "Blood Lust." . . .

From "A Wild Sowing: The Short Stories of Liam O'Flaherty," *Review of English Literature* 4 (July 1963): 108–13. Reprinted with permission of the journal's former editor, Professor A. Norman Jeffares.

Some of the pieces ("The Wave" and "The Rockfish," for example) contain little more than description: this is characteristic of the later O'Flaherty. A further forecast is apparent in "Wolf Lonigan's Death," in which a lurid miasma prophetic of *The Informer* (1925) appears. Here one must remember O'Flaherty's reported liking for Hemingway and Dreiser, as well as his belief that good writing "must come out of reality" and "the only true mysticism comes through reality." His "mysticism" is, however, sometimes confused with the kind of sentimentality that leads to theatricalism, poor taste, clichés: I am thinking of such work as "Beauty," in which the sight of two trees stirs symbolical religious sentimentality in a man, with revulsion against a seductive woman just in time to prevent his being unfaithful to his fiancée; he staggers and groans—the rejected woman *hisses* "you cur"—and he even ends by hugging and kissing one of the trees!

The twenty-nine stories of *The Tent*—O'Flaherty's titles are as literal as they are simple in designation—include three of striking quality: the title-piece, "Milking Time" and "The Wild Goat's Kid." "The Tent" concerns an . . . episode of brutal life raw enough to appeal to O'Flaherty. The other two stories, in contrast, are wholly charming. Indeed they are almost perfect idylls which represent a precisely opposite type of appeal to this man of extremes. "Milking Time" . . . parallels "Spring Sowing"; but "The Wild Goat's Kid" is less easily compared. . . . Nothing could be simpler; little in all O'Flaherty is more lyrically moving.

For the rest, there is . . . much description of the physical characteristics and responses of animals, constant concern with "the short and simple annals of the poor," some sardonic handling of callous priests in "The Outcast" and "Offerings." . . .

. . . There are also the unpalatable figures of "The Strange Disease" and "The Child of God" in *The Mountain Tavern*. O'Flaherty exhibits a sensitivity to seasonal change as acute as that of a lyric poet, and is deeply concerned with horror in such stories as "Civil War" and "The Terrorist," and even with non-human cruelty in "The Wounded Cormorant" and "The Jealous Hens." But his range is now richer and wider than that he explored in *Spring Sowing*, though equally sparse in humorous content. One story—"Poor People"—is a picture of poverty and suffering so rending as to be at once story and almost-unendurable social document. "Mother and Son" comes as a relief after this; it is a story which is suspiciously suggestive of the whoppers O'Flaherty . . .

used to tell his mother when he was a child. There are the technical slips which are not unusual in this author ("Her cheeks had a rosy flush like a young girl"); but these are less impressive than the unflagging drive of vitality and the freshness of observation ("a slight snapping sound like the end of a dog's yawn"). Ultimately this is a book that counts.

A similar judgement must be accorded *The Mountain Tavern and Other Stories*. . . . Happily there is less sentimentality in the concern with animals than usual in O'Flaherty. There is "The Fairy Goose," a charming thing with the qualities appropriate to the suggestion of its title; "Birth," concerned with the birth of a calf and with country tenderness; "Red Barbara," the tale of a sensual, earthy, indolent widow wed to a gentle weaver whose impotence leads to a sort of madness before death; "The Oar," a masterpiece of eerie and wild description of the struggle of two fishing curraghs to get to shore in a storm, and of Red Bartly's haunting by a helplessly passed face and upraised oar in the sea; and there is the touching, and wholly unsentimental, "The Letter" in which a twenty-pound cheque from a daughter long silent in America is accompanied by a heartbroken letter revealing that she is a prostitute. And for ironic amusement, there is "The Fall of Joseph Timmins" in which the husband of an arid, over sanctimonious woman is caught by his disapproved-of nephew while trying to seduce a maid—and has got to become obliging.

Two Lovely Beasts and Other Stories represents a somewhat milder brew. Of the twenty tales, seven or eight are up to O'Flaherty's normal standard; but only one—"Grey Seagull," reflecting its author's preoccupation with horse-racing—seems superlative.

. . . The prose is muscular, so nearly completely free of clichés that it is almost startling to come on "foam-laced" and "eyes . . . as blue as the sea." Luckily this prose preserves hints of the O'Flaherty who is sensitive to the pathos of fierce age, affectionately observant of beast as well as man, and capable of poetry in individual dry-point in his response to nature. All this compensates for some apparent weakening in vitality.

O'Flaherty is an author whose miscellaneous achievement is critically somewhat disturbing. The dark tides sweeping through his best novels and short stories—the tumult and sometimes the uncouthness—can be very exciting; the O'Flaherty who counts is both gripping and panoramic; he is never a man to say nay to life. On the other hand, he generally lacks any impressive degree of real divination; his apparent lyricism is sometimes suggestive of the bogus—is too often merely a rush, rather than a grace, of wings; he is frequently tautological; and his minute descriptions and psychological meanderings can become very tedious, as can his seeming obsession with cruelty. Nor does he induce the unfaltering conviction that he is an artist who is never satisfied with anything but the precisely right word. Probably the *Times Literary Supplement* (19 April 1934) was correct to suggest that "it is not unreasonable to surmise that his powerful and primitive imagination has been forced too rapidly, and therefore thwarted, by the modern cult of literary violence and exaggeration." Yet, despite his failing, he remains well worth reading.

Paul A. Doyle

O'Flaherty's generally plain, flat, and rough style is especially noticeable in his short stories. Like Dreiser's writing, O'Flaherty's style usually appears to be laboring; it struggles; it is a sort of hewing-out-of-rock prose in which the hammering and the hard resistance of the words are apparent. The prose is undistinguished, and a decided preference for language that is hackneyed is evident. Clichés abound: "White—like the teeth of a Negro," "as quick as a cat," "pure like a young virgin," "he smiled like a happy child and his head swam." In O'Flaherty's superior stories, the clichés are fewer; the roughness blends well with the peasant and rural subject matter; and the earnest, accurate, detailed observation lifts the material to a more meaningful level of accomplishment and impact.

O'Flaherty's writing tone is generally bitter, grim, even sardonic. Rarely does he use humor; and, when he attempts comedy as, for example, in "The Stolen Ass," the humor is usually of the obvious tall-tale type. . . .

O'Flaherty, from time to time, makes use of satire to ridicule aspects

From *Liam O'Flaherty* (New York: Twayne Publishers, 1971), 53–59. © 1971 by Twayne Publishers, a division of G. K. Hall & Co. Reprinted by permission of the publisher and Professor Doyle.

of Irish life and behavior which he finds offensive. For example, he satirizes the clergy in several stories, as in "Offerings" and "The Strange Disease," and he attacks such abuses as profiteering and injustice on the part of storekeepers. But his satire possesses a gnarled heavy-handedness and is too pat and obvious didactic preachment to be successful. Indeed, the only effective satire O'Flaherty wrote in his career is "The Fairy Goose," which owes much of its felicitousness to a lightness achieved by the use of fantasy and colorful imagination. . . .

"The Cow's Death" is typical of the animal sketches. The cow's appearance and reactions after having given birth to a stillborn calf are described so closely that the reader participates as an on-the-scene observer. . . .

Like the rockfish story, O'Flaherty's "The Conger Eel" offers another lucky creature of nature. . . . The eel is finally grasped and lifted by the younger of the fishermen; but, before he can be killed, he slips free and falls into the sea, escaping to the depths of his lair. Not so fortunate is the wounded cormorant in a story of that title. When a stone near the edge of the cliff of Clogher Mor is accidentally dislodged by a grazing goat, the rock missile crashes down on several cormorants who are resting on a large rock below the cliff. When the leg of one of the cormorants is broken by a stone that falls on top of him, . . . [the other members of the flock attack him]. The savage instinct of the pack causes them to hound and bring a weaker member to doom. . . .

It is unquestionably true that O'Flaherty has periods of failure in trying to convey the thoughts or feelings of animal life, but he is more often successful than not. When a false note intrudes, it seems so possible and feasible that, in general, the questionable exaggerations and imaginative reflections are excusable in the light of the over-all effectiveness of the story. . . .

A total picture develops, then, of a writer who has obvious faults and weaknesses but who, in his finest work, can write short narratives so "compact, so deeply felt, so instinctive . . . so surely conceived."

John Zneimer

When I first began reading the works of Liam O'Flaherty, it seemed so obvious that he was a writer with the same sort of awareness as Dostoevsky, Sartre, Camus, or the film-maker Ingmar Bergman that I was surprised to learn that this was not the common interpretation. Despite O'Flaherty's debt to Dostoevsky (which is always recognized), critics and commentators have tended to see him according to the Irish measure—as a naturalist, a realist, a social critic or historian, or a voice of things Irish, an acquaintance of Yeats, George Russell, and Sean O'Casey. And in this assessment O'Flaherty usually ends up somehow as an Irishman *manqué*.

I respect the opinion that it takes an Irishman to understand the Irish, and I know that what I set out to do here is undertaken at considerable risk—I also respect the barbed Irish wit. But granting that much about Irish literature is accessible only to Irishmen, much also is obscured by a characteristic Irish bias. My intention here is to show that if O'Flaherty were seen less as an Irishman and more as a man, many of the "problems" associated with his work would be illuminated or eliminated. . . . [H]is place belongs as much in an existentialist tradition as it does in an Irish tradition. . . .

To turn from O'Flaherty's novels to his short stories seems to be a move into another world. . . . Some marvelous transformation has taken place. It is not just that the setting has changed, although indeed it has. The novels tend to be set in town, in the cities, or, more important, among people who aspire and interact. The short stories turn to the country, to animals, and to nature. The society that appears is a part of nature. The characters are rough-hewn from Aran rock. The whole tone has changed. The same vocabulary does not seem to apply. The novels can be described by a vocabulary of heat. The short stories can be described by light. Their surface is cold and shimmering. If the

From *The Literary Vision of Liam O'Flaherty* (Syracuse, N.Y.: Syracuse University Press, 1970), vii, 146–47, 157–60, 174–76. Reprinted by permission of Syracuse University Press. © 1970 by Syracuse University Press.

novels are marked by violence and melodrama and fury, O'Flaherty's short stories are best marked by their qualities of calmness, simplicity, and detachment. Or that is the impression so strong that it takes an effort of mind in retrospect to see that the violence is still there. A cow plunges over a cliff. A man crushes a fish to a pulp to relieve his blood lust. A water hen awaits the outcome of a furious struggle to see who will be her mate. Everywhere there is the conflict of nature and the anguish of those who are a part of nature. Yet all *is* changed. And this change must be explored. . . .

. . . [T]he stories themselves would seem to offer little clue to what this change has been. There is an air of inevitability, an austerity and simplicity that seem to defy analysis. The stories do not appear to be constructions, that is, arrangements of details to achieve an esthetic effect. Nor is there any meaning in the sense that the details are the garb of any systematic intellectual arrangement. The stories cannot be called symbolic as the term has come to be used in criticism, with a *this* representing *that* relationship of details and events. Indeed, the contemporary scholar who has become accustomed to approaching short stories as an intellectual challenge or problem in need of scholarly interpretation or explication will find no rich mine in O'Flaherty.

Simplicity is the keynote. The short stories do not *mean;* they *are*. . . . Now, as might be expected, this has significant consequences in artistic form and explains the characteristic form of an O'Flaherty short story. Take "The Rockfish." . . . The story is short—not 1,500 words. And it is simple—a fish is almost caught. That is really all there is to it. . . . It is almost easier to describe what the story is not than what it is. There are no characters in any common sense in which the term is used. The fisherman is merely there. Except that he is large, there is no special quality about the fish. The story is not a vehicle for the author's descriptions of nature. What little happens is not important as far as any sense of plot is concerned. Nothing is symbolic of anything. There are no hidden meanings, no allegory. The author makes no observations about the meaning of the experience. If any conventional expectations about what stories should be or contain are used as a criterion, the reader would find himself among those persons of inferior taste who would prefer "Selling Pigs."

What is expressed is the vision, the kinship and oneness of the author with the natural scene in the most direct expression possible. The order of events is natural, inevitable. . . . Apparently, the author does not arrange the parts. Each event occurs after every other. The connective is *then*, not *while* or *meanwhile*. Each sentence either depicts a static scene or advances the action. Nothing is described as being contemporaneous, for this would require the presence of an author holding one set of actions in abeyance while another took place. There is no backward or simultaneous flow. From the moment the lead hits the water until the fish is free all motion is forward and relentless, like the ticking of a clock.

As the special relationship of the author to his material must eliminate the complexities of time (and with it those words used to denote these complexities) so the careful elimination of author intervention in any form must eliminate intellectual and logical complexities. No relationships are stated through the use of logical words like *though* or *because*. No such words appear, for these are intellectual "author" words not a part of the natural scene which contains no intellect probing beneath the surface. That depicted is pure vision. No author is there explaining relationships, standing outside the material and seeing the parts relate to each other temporally or causally. . . .

. . . The characteristic form is primarily the result of the author, because of the nature of that which he is attempting to express, deliberately removing all sense of himself from the story. And this is carried to a degree much further than mere technical objectivity. Not only is the *I* removed, but all sense of narrator is removed. The objectivity goes further even than the dramatic, for in a dramatic presentation there is still the sense of a deliberate arrangement of speeches for preconceived purposes. In "The Rockfish" there appear to be no preconceived purposes. The intellect is removed by eliminating the characteristic intellectual sense of causality and complex time relationships. With this go all complex plot relationships and character analyses and relationships. The simple sentences laid end to end, clearly and separately, while perhaps the most obvious characteristic of the style, are not the cause of the simplicity but the result of this other process. The spiritual insight, experienced so intensely and personally as to be ineffable, is expressed so objectively that the author goes to unusual means to eliminate every possible trace of his presence. And through this artifice, in a full circle, is expressed just that which is most significant in the spiritual insight: the fusion of the black soul-intellect-divisive force into the whole man who loses all sense of self in a union and harmony with the ongoing, unquesting life force and process of nature. . . .

His correspondence with Garnett would seem to indicate that O'Flaherty did not attach much importance to his short stories. . . . It is not just that he is not the best judge of his own work. It is natural that the novels fill his mind. Not only do they offer the greatest opportunity for fame and wealth, but they are more interesting intellectually. He may announce enthusiastically to Garnett the completion of one story or another, but there is little more to talk about, because by their very nature the stories are not intellectually interesting. After the process of creation they *exist*. They do not contain ideas. They are not controversial. They contain no complex problems of plot and character development that fill his letters to Garnett concerning *The Informer* and *The Black Soul*. But O'Flaherty's more unerring "instinct," which O'Connor sets above his judgment, keeps the perspective aright. Out of the spiritual crisis described in *Shame the Devil*, where O'Flaherty discovers what and who he is, emerges not a novel, but "The Caress." This is what he writes when he accepts in understanding and humility his lot as a writer. *Shame the Devil* explores and exhausts openly and directly the spiritual quest that lay at the basis of the novels preceding it. When the vanity and arrogance and rhetoric are burned away, he writes a short story.

Helene O'Connor

O'Flaherty's stories should find an appreciative new audience in contemporary readers who have recently begun to recognize the importance of ecology. . . .

His stories often depict the crucial ecological moment—the moment when the existing balance of nature is disturbed and a new balance is achieved. These can be the primal moments of life—birth, death, a sudden battle or accident that alters irrevocably human or animal relationships. The story can even describe an inanimate disturbance, as in "The Wave" where a giant wave suddenly erodes a cliff, and a new

From "Liam O'Flaherty: Literary Ecologist," *Éire-Ireland: A Journal of Irish Studies* 7, no. 2 (Summer 1972): 47–48, 49–50, 51, 52, 53–54. Reprinted by permission of the editor of *Éire-Ireland* and the Irish American Cultural Institute, St. Paul, Minnesota.

equilibrium is established; this is the repeated and distinctive pattern of O'Flaherty's stories.

For O'Flaherty the significant situation is the one in which man or animal is guided by his most basic instinct, when he is following his innate imperatives for survival. In the basic biological patterns of life man differs from animals as one highly intelligent species differs from lower ones. The patterns of behavior are on a higher level but are similar. The chief biological drive is, of course, that for survival. Contributory to this are hunger, reproduction, flight and territorial drives. To differing degrees and in differing ways both men and animals are subject to these powerful drives. For one who views man primarily as a species of animal, as O'Flaherty does, the situations involving these various drives are bound to be strikingly similar whether man or animal is concerned.

Thus, O'Flaherty's simple peasant tales are not just anecdotes nor are his stories of animals even merely adventures. They express with every precise detail the author's recognition that biological drives determine most of the activity of men and animals on earth. He sees in the daily activity of men and animals the elemental patterns of life and its ultimate meaning—survival. This philosophical undercurrent imbues even the simplest of O'Flaherty's stories with an almost inexplicable significance and weight. . . .

. . . As a true ecologist O'Flaherty like Stapleton, a character in his novel *Insurrection,* is in "revolt against the idea that man is the center of the universe."[1] Peasants fulfill the oldest behavior patterns on earth. O'Flaherty's respect for the peasant and his awareness of his historical and ecological significance pervade each story.

The quiet dignity he achieves is best illustrated by an examination of the title story of his first collection, "Spring Sowing." . . . The plot could not be more simple, the characterization is superficial, yet the impact of the story is profound. O'Flaherty has compressed into his brief narrative a sense of the endless cycle of the years, the earth and our lives on it. . . .

. . . O'Flaherty subtly stresses the relentless ecology of peasant life. At the same moment that the couple are mastering the earth and savoring its promise for them, they are also aware of its tyranny over them—their very lives are dependent on its bounty. . . .

. . . "Red Barbara" is one of the best of O'Flaherty's many stories on fertility. . . .

The story, told impassively by one of the villagers, is another peasant tale that affirms more strongly than any text the ecological virtue of fertility. . . .

O'Flaherty treats an inversion of this theme—sterility—in two memorable stories with similar symbolic figures. Both "The Wedding" and "The Stream" contain the character of a withered crone. . . . Women in his ecological (if unliberated) view are born to be mates.

. . . "Birth" describes the process and emotions that man shares with even bovine creatures. Man's tolerance for the lower species, he implies, should be based on more than utility.

O'Flaherty is intensely interested in animals, but he is also interested in the earth itself. He is absorbed by the inexorable ecology of the universe which changes everything in a matter of moments. A story that epitomizes this interest is "The Wave." No one but O'Flaherty would have written it; it is, in fact, hardly a story at all. One critic referred to it as a vignette.[2] If one were not aware of O'Flaherty's interest in ecology as a dramatic force, the story might seem like an exercise in descriptive writing. . . .

Seán Ó Faoláin once commented about these stories that "one has the feeling that O'Flaherty has his ear to the earth, listening quietly."[3] The image is an appropriate tribute to O'Flaherty's considerable ecological knowledge. One can only guess at the hours he has spent in observations of animals in their natural environment. The authenticity conveyed could have been achieved only through long and painstaking vigil. His short stories affirm that it was time well spent.

Notes

1. (Boston: Little, Brown, 1951), 204.
2. Michael H. Murray, "Liam O'Flaherty and the Speaking Voice," *Studies in Short Fiction*, 5 (Winter 1968): 155–56.
3. "Don Quixote O'Flaherty," *London Mercury* 37 (December 1937): 174.

George O'Brien

By eschewing thought and dispensing with self-absorbed protagonists, O'Flaherty's short fiction dwells on the most telling artistic feature of the novels, their immediacy of impact and sense of presence. It is generally agreed that O'Flaherty is the greatest Irish short-story writer. His unique innovation was to conceive of stories (or, bearing their superbly visual effects in mind, to draw sketches) largely devoid of human beings—cameos of fish, birds, and other undomesticated creatures: "The Rockfish," "The Wild Swan." But even stories such as "Two Lovely Beasts" and "Red Barbara" which have thematic echoes of the novels tend to portray their characters as natural phenomena, largely immune from the trials of consciousness. As in the novels, the quality of O'Flaherty's stories is very erratic. At their best, however, they achieve a rapturous attentiveness more artistically complete than anything in the longer works. . . . O'Flaherty's existential and primitivist concerns, and the expressionistic vigour of his prose, ensure him of a small place in the history of Modernism.

From *Novelists and Prose Writers*, ed. James Vinson (London: Macmillan, 1979), 927. Reprinted by permission of Macmillan Press. © 1979 Macmillan Press.

Vivian Mercier

What happened to O'Flaherty after 1937, the publication date of *Famine*? Why did the creative drive that had produced twelve novels, three volumes of short stories, and four other full-length books in fourteen years culminate in a masterpiece and then peter out almost entirely

From "Man against Nature: The Novels of Liam O'Flaherty," *Wascana Review* 1, no. 2 (1966): 44–45. Reprinted by permission of the editors of *Wascana Review*.

after two further, inferior novels? The explanation, in my opinion, must be provided by the biographer rather than the literary critic.

Until O'Flaherty finds his Ellmann I can only hazard a guess. Remembering the huge number of O'Flaherty's characters, major and minor, who end their lives hopelessly insane, I would suggest that his great creative outpouring was a form of mental therapy. Shell-shocked in World War I and the victim of one or more nervous breakdowns thereafter, O'Flaherty may have visited upon his deranged characters the fate that he feared for himself. Having grown more stable as he grew older, he may have lost his fear of madness only to find that he had exorcized his creative demon at the same time.

My assumption—for it is no more than that—of O'Flaherty's increased mental stability in recent years is based upon many of his later short stories and especially upon my favorite among them, "The Blow," with its compassion for the weak and its gentler view of nature. Such work suggests a faint possibility that the older, mellower O'Flaherty might have begun a new and greater career in fiction after 1950, the publication date of *Insurrection*. In fact, he did break new ground in 1953 with the publication of his first volume in Gaelic, *Dúil*, a collection of short stories. The five previously uncollected stories in *The Stories of Liam O'Flaherty*—"The Hawk," "The Blow," "The Mirror," "Desire," "The Post Office"—are all to be found in the Gaelic volume, and the last four of them represent the mellower vein that I detect in his later work.

But it is hard for a writer to begin over again when he is already middle-aged and famous, to say as Yeats did, "Myself I must remake." In the absence of any new work by O'Flaherty since 1956, we must content ourselves with rereading *Famine, Skerrett*, perhaps one or two other novels, and almost all the short stories.

Vivian Mercier

He is a native speaker of Gaelic and therefore born into the oral tradition, but, paradoxically, he is also the least oral in his approach to narrative [of Irish writers]. I agree with Frank O'Connor's statement that O'Flaherty's English "lacks the distinction and beauty of his Gaelic,"[1] but—even in Gaelic O'Flaherty writes far more for the eye than he does for the ear or the speaking voice. Why is this? One's first answer must refer to individual temperament: O'Flaherty writes as naturally for the eye as the mature Joyce wrote for the ear; it is no accident that *The Informer* provided the outline for one of the most admired films ever made in Hollywood. I could point to thousands of passages in O'Flaherty's novels and short stories which are seen through the eye of a camera; two notable examples occur to me at once, the murder scene in *The Assassin* and the short story called "The Landing," though every one of his animal stories is also conceived in cinematic terms.[2] O'Flaherty resembles no single writer so closely as he does the late great documentary film director Robert Flaherty, who filmed so many of his namesake's subjects in *Man of Aran*.

I would suggest a second reason, connected with the revival of Gaelic, to explain why O'Flaherty is so exempt from the influence of the oral tradition: he is *literate* in Gaelic, and doubtless has been so since his earliest years in elementary school. In contrast, Carleton was completely illiterate in Gaelic until the day he died; some of the phonetic equivalents for Gaelic phrases that he uses in his stories might well make a Celtic scholar weep. Whereas a Carleton, by his own avowal, is constantly transferring oral Gaelic into written English, an O'Flaherty may translate visual images directly into the written symbols of whichever language he happens to be using at the moment.

Notes

1. *New York Times Book Review*, 10 June 1956, 20.
2. *The Assassin* (London: Cape, 1928), chap. 18.

Reprinted from "The Irish Short Story and Oral Tradition," in *The Celtic Cross: Studies in Irish Culture and Literature*, ed. Ray B. Browne, William John Rosselli, and John Loftus (West Lafayette, Ind.: Purdue University Press, 1964), 105–6.

Angeline A. Hampton
(Angeline A. Kelly)

O'Flaherty's strong visual imagination as evidenced in these stories, and his use of colour, sound, punctuation and repetition may be related to the author's oral heritage. . . .

. . . There are numerous passages of description in O'Flaherty's peasant stories which testify to his powerful visual imagination. . . . That the visual is important to O'Flaherty is also shown in his deliberate use of colour, as in "The Oar" where the bream have "gauzy red lips," "the enchanted light" is described as red over a black sea. . . . The vivid description of small actions, of gestures, often serves as a pointer to the characters' inner state of mind. . . . In many stories O'Flaherty demonstrates his strong visual inclination by the variation of camera angle and distance in his descriptive writing.

In his early stories and in the animal stories, sound plays an important part and often, like colour, it is used to create atmosphere. In O'Flaherty's later work much of this aural description is replaced by dialogue. . . . The importance given to sound in O'Flaherty's early work indicates that he often intends his stories to be heard with the inner ear, but sometimes he also wishes to appeal to the outer ear and some of his work begs to be read aloud. This impression was confirmed when in conversation with the author I asked why he had not written more poetry and he replied "What is poetry?" and recited the opening paragraph of "The Oar" as follows:

> Beneath tall cliffs,
> two anchored curraghs swung,
> their light prows bobbing on the gentle waves.
> Their tarred sides shone in the moonlight,
> In each, three stooping figures sat on narrow seats,

From "Liam O'Flaherty's Short Stories—Visual and Aural Effects," *English Studies* 55, no. 5 (October 1974): 440–44, 446–47. Reprinted by permission of the editors of *English Studies*. A version of this article also appeared in Kelly's *Liam O'Flaherty the Storyteller* (1976).

155

their arms resting on the frail sides,
their red-backed hands fingering long lines,
that swam, white, through the deep dark water.

This is a visual passage written not only to impress the inner ear, but with oral intent, as the heavy punctuation shows.

O'Flaherty uses punctuation to control the tempo as well as the meaning of his words, and attention to his use of punctuation will often give us a clue as to how he intends a passage to be read. . . .

. . . Some of O'Flaherty's repetition is unconscious and due to carelessness. In "The Sinner" for example, evidence of stylistic weakness occurs not only in the use of clichés (such as "sorely tempted," "boon companion," "a transport of passion" or "wreathed with smiles"), but there is also a threefold repetition of "because" just before Julia jumps out of bed and rings for Sally. . . . In general, however, it is easy to distinguish between haphazard repetition which contributes nothing and may sound clumsy, and the deliberate repetition used for emphasis, for its euphonic value, or to reproduce speech patterns.

Deliberate repetition to create emphasis, when it is used in a passage of narrative, can take the form of a keyword as with the word "crooning" at the beginning of "Milking Time," used in connection with the woman herself, her voice, her lips, her words and her dreaming thoughts. This is not only an associative word symbolic of the woman's future state as a mother, but it also acts as a musical refrain to colour the mood at the beginning of the story. . . .

In "The Oar" we find this striking passage: "Suddenly it became more silent. . . . From afar a bellowing noise came and then a wave shimmered over a smooth rock quite near. Tchee . . . ee . . . ee, it said." It is obvious that O'Flaherty is here again drawing attention to the sound effects of the words and that he uses punctuation, repetition and alliteration to do so. . . .

Were all O'Flaherty's repetitive refrains to voice the feelings, or describe the behaviour, of his peasant characters, we might presume that by using them he is merely being faithful to the traditional habits of life and speech of his people. But the fact that he also uses descriptive narrative repetition in "Red Barbara" and "The Mountain Tavern" points, I believe, to a subconscious as well as a deliberate reason for his using this literary device. O'Flaherty came from a community with a strong oral tradition and his liking for repetition, which he shows at all stages of his literary development, may have been subconsciously affected by the Gaelic story-telling he heard as a child, for a characteristic of the folktale is to use formulaic repeated phrases to create a special rhetorical effect. Liam's brother Tom mentions that in his youth the Aran islanders had stories for each season, and describes how the villagers used to gather every evening in the O'Flaherty home and pass the time telling stories and discussing various subjects, often well into the night.

In his discussion of the relationship between the Irish short story and oral tradition Vivian Mercier favours the view that oral literature has had a direct influence, but he does not find O'Flaherty to be, on the whole, a very "oral" writer.

"The Black Mare" is the most traditionally oral of all O'Flaherty's stories. The protagonist/narrator addresses himself to the interlocutor in person, calling him "Stranger, who has been in many lands across the sea." The story of this exceptional mare is in the Gaelic tradition of the wondertale. There is a high incidence of imagery, some of it a typical Christian/pagan mixture. The story-teller uses proverbs twice, "talk of beauty today, talk of death tomorrow," and "the laugh is the herald of the sigh" introducing anticipation—an oral tradition—for in the end the beautiful horse is destroyed. . . .

In O'Flaherty, then, we shall find both the vivid imagination which characterizes the short story and the folktale, and undeniable traces of his origins in an "oral" community.

It is true that O'Flaherty's stories are an art form intended for the printed page, but his frequent descriptive aural as well as visual effects, his use of punctuation, repetition of words and phrases, all point to the fact that, in some of his stories at least, he expects his reader to listen and not only to visualise his stories, and that his aural and visual imagination were both active when he wrote them.

Brendan Kennelly

His best stories are about wild creatures, and why the distinctive O'Flaherty poetry occurs most of all in those stories. . . . "Wild Stallions" falls naturally into verse. If we listen to its rhythms, the varying cool impassioned flow of its sympathies, its unfolding of anticipation, conflict and resolution, we find ourselves in the company not of a modern writer of short stories but of a bardic teller of tales, a narrator for whom the disclosure of marvels is as natural and inevitable as the ear for the rhythms of city-talk is natural to James Joyce. Here is the opening of "Wild Stallions."

> As he stood over his grazing herd,
> on a hillock near the northern wall
> of his lofty mountain glen,
> the golden stallion's mane and tail
> looked almost white in the radiant light of dawn.
> At the centre of his forehead,
> a small star shone like a jewel.

This beautiful rhythm is maintained right through the story which has a fierce sexual pulse. The final clash of the two wild stallions, which will decide the sexual supremacy for which they struggle to the death, shows O'Flaherty's poetry in full epic flight.

> Neighing hoarsely in his throat,
> the invader cantered forward slowly
> with his head bowed. The golden stallion
> stood his ground on widespread legs,
> mustering the last remnants of his strength,
> until the enemy swerved at close quarters
> to deliver a broadside.

Reprinted from "Liam O'Flaherty: The Unchained Storm, a View of His Short Stories," in *The Irish Short Story*, ed. Patrick Rafroidi and Terence Brown (Gerrards Cross, Buckinghamshire, England: Colin Smythe, 1979), 180–81. © 1979 by Presses Universitaires de Lille and Colin Smythe Ltd.

158

Then he rose and brought his forelegs down
with great force.
Struck above the kidneys,
the grey uttered a shrill cry and fell.
While rolling away, a second blow on the spine
made him groan and shudder from head to tail.
With his glazed eyes wide open,
he turned over on his back,
swung his neck from side to side
and snapped his jaws without known purpose
in the urgent agony of death.

It is worth noting here that "Wild Stallions" is an excellent example of the crisp, definite way in which O'Flaherty often manages to finish his stories. He rarely lingers indulgently in the drama he has created, or dallies complacently in lyrical climax. The ending of "Wild Stallions" is as clean as the cut of the sharpest axe. The golden stallion, a maimed victor pursued by wild predators, is briefly defended by his mares but "Then two of the mountain lions / broke through the circle / and brought him down."

John Broderick

There is a hardness about O'Flaherty, a true ring of steel, which one is conscious of in the work of all great writers. Unlike Hemingway, with whom he has sometimes been compared, there is no soft centre in his best work. Of all the Irish writers who have written in English he is the most Gaelic in style and temperament. Indeed his stories sometimes read like translations from the Irish; and for all I know they may well be. Now, the Irish are not a sentimental people, like the Americans and the English. They are clear-eyed, realistic, and hard as nails, in spite of a certain superficial sweetness and an elaborate code of manners. But they have never lacked courage; above all the ability to survive. Those people, and they are not all visitors, newly established planters or tourists, who think of the Irish as a race of easy-going

Reprinted from "Liam O'Flaherty: A Partial View," *Hibernia*, 19 December 1969, 17.

charmers, given to the philosophy of dolce far niente, have clearly not read their O'Flaherty. Consider his treatment of animals. His animal stories, which are justly famous, are light years apart from the cosy English attitude of attributing human characteristics to all manner of beasts. They identify themselves with them in a way which would be less alarming if it were also less suburban.

O'Flaherty never makes this mistake. His approach to animals is completely unsentimental, which greatly heightens his natural sympathy and understanding; and the result is marvellously vivid, clear cut and vital. Hardly any other writer has equalled him in this particular field.

Eoghan Ó hAnluain

In 1925 following the publication of "Bás na Bó" (The Cow's Death) in *Fainne an Lae* Pádraic Ó Conaire, then in Galway, wrote to his friend F. R. Higgins in Dublin telling him how pleased and excited he was to see a story in Irish by Liam Ó Flaithearta.

"Tell him to keep it up," he wrote.

O'Flaherty did in fact publish a few more stories that year but 20 years were to pass before he published again in Irish. The stories from these two periods made up his single volume in Irish, *Dúil*, published in 1953.

To have come to an awareness of contemporary writing in Irish in the late fifties and discover *Dúil* was exhilarating. It is no exaggeration to say that the book played a great part in establishing the credentials of the revival of Irish writing in the forties and fifties. Its qualities are remarkable. The stories are simple but profound in their impact and this is achieved by the keenest observations of men, women and beasts presented with vivid accuracy.

On hearing of the death of a cherished writer one's impulse is to turn

From "A Writer Who Bolstered the Irish Revival," *Irish Times*, 8 September 1984, 7. Reprinted by permission of the editor of the *Irish Times* and Eoghan Ó hAnluain of the Department of Modern Irish at University College, Dublin.

to his writing. One story in *Dúil* which never ceases to engage me is "An Chulaith Nua" (The New Suit)—the excitement of a boy who longs for his first new suit. O'Flaherty presents through the amazed and anxious eyes of the child the mysterious rituals of shearing, bleaching, teasing, carding, spinning and weaving. The authority of language in description and liveliness in dialogue, and in telling of a good story with a good punchline remains a wonder of perfection. He focuses his vision on a simple event that conveys a whole way of life. While one is entertained by the characters in the foreground one is aware of a tapestry of immemorial conventions being unfolded. And this with the greatest economy of language.

When reviewing a book of Mairtin Ó Cadhain, O'Flaherty wrote (I translate), "Words are a writer's raw material which he should regard as precious and use sparingly . . . the art of good writing is knowing what is superfluous." This is an apt description of his own stories in *Dúil*. He shunned the cliché; the proverbial turn of phrase, and the freshness achieved has remained. Looking through my own battered copy which I have used as a text book over the years I am struck by the annotations—each reading with students producing new insights to his mastery as a writer.

Shortly after the publication of *Dúil*, Seán Ó Riordáin wrote of it in his journal (I translate) "I have read some stories by Liam O'Flaherty and sensed that some living things had been caught between the covers. If you held a robin and felt it quiver in your hands you would know what I felt reading Liam O'Flaherty's Irish."

Unfortunately, Liam O'Flaherty did not continue to write in Irish after the publication of *Dúil*. While editing in the late sixties I approached him in the hope that he might write again in Irish but on the two occasions we met under the Cusack Stand in Croke Park he did not want to discuss the matter and talked mostly of the great three-in-a-row Galway football team.

But *Dúil* survives—like so much else in literature in Irish, early or late, a unique and marvellous book.

Tomás de Bhaldraithe

O'Flaherty is probably the only native Irish speaker in our time who gained a world-wide reputation for his writing in English. He has published about twenty short stories in Irish, and an English version of most of them. . . . A comparison of the two versions of each story should prove an interesting linguistic and stylistic exercise. Such a comparison may not always give clear results. Someone who has been writing in English all his life, even when his first language is Irish, is often prone to use *béarlachas* (Irish influenced by English idiom). This is particularly true in the case of prose, because of the almost complete break during the last century in traditional prose-writing (in contrast to traditional verse-writing), and of the consequent scarcity of good modern prose writers. . . .

In studying the internal evidence, then, for an English original in the case of O'Flaherty's stories, it must be kept in mind that he did very little writing in his native Irish; and, therefore, that when his Irish style appears unnatural or based on English idiom, it need not necessarily follow that he was translating. On the other hand, where the meaning is quite clear in the English version, and unintelligible in the Irish, it is likely that English was the original, or that the Irish suffered badly at the hands of a proof-reader. Take, for example, the following passage from *Poor People* (Cape, 1962): "The edge of the sea was full of seaweed, a great load spilling from the deep, red, slime-covered, dribbling in with every wave that broke slowly murmuring in the darkness of the dawn." A literal translation of the Irish [from "Daoine Bochta" in *Dúil*] would be: "The edge of the sea was full of seaweed, a heavy load being spilled on the red world, cloudy, folding in (coming back in?), frond by frond."

From "Liam O'Flaherty—Translator (?)," *Éire-Ireland: A Journal of Irish Studies* 3, no. 2 (Summer 1968): 149–53. Reprinted by permission of the editor of *Éire-Ireland*, the Irish American Cultural Institute in St. Paul, Minnesota, and Professor de Bhaldraithe.

The first Irish version . . . had ". . . *ar an domhain dearg*" (on the red deep). Perhaps the discrepancy has not to do with translation in this case, but with proof-reading. If ". . . *ar an domhan dearg, scamallach, ag filleadh isteach* . . ." were replaced by "*as an domhain, dearg, ramallach, ag silleadh isteach* . . ." the Irish and English versions would correspond exactly.

It is clear from the above example that until a careful examination of all the versions, both Irish and English are made, it will not be possible to say definitely from internal evidence which are translations and which are originals.

I take here "Teangabháil" . . . and "The Touch" . . . as an example of O'Flaherty's translations from Irish, since it is fairly certain from internal evidence that the original was in Irish, as well as from the facts that it was written in answer to a request by the Irish-language periodical *Comhar,* and that it appeared in Irish before it appeared in English.

In the first English version . . . O'Flaherty has modified both the theme, the style, and consequently the whole atmosphere of the story. The Irish version is the story of two young lovers who let their love be known to each other for the first time during "the touch." Immediately afterwards when the young man shows himself a coward when faced by his employer, the girl's father, the girl loses her respect and love for him. In fact, O'Flaherty overstresses the cowardice of the young man in the Irish version where he refers to it at three different points. . . . In the first English version none of these extracts occur. Neither is there any mention of cowardice.

In this English version the father attacks Beartla because of his inefficient work, and not because of his dealings with his daughter. . . . The English version, by omitting Cáit's sudden revulsion and rejection of the coward, becomes the simple well-worn story of a wealthy father who prevents his daughter marrying a pauper.

There is another significant difference between the two versions. The English version makes Cáit treat and speak affectionately to the horse "'Easy now, treasure' Cáit whispered to her. 'Take it easy, darling. Preoil! My little hag!,'" which does not appear in the original Irish.

The difference in style in the translation is striking. Where Beartla says "*Deabhail gháirsiúla! Ba cheart daoine mar sin a chaitheamh le aill!*" (Loose-mouthed devils! People like that should be thrown over the cliff), in English he is made to say "Loose-mouthed devils! May the swine be maimed and gouged!" *"Dar lán an leabhair"*[1] *a deir fear acu 'Dá mbeinnse aonraic inniu is ar a méar bheadh tnúthán agam le fáinne a chur"* ("By the book! . . ." is translated by "By the blade of the lance! . . .") . . . *"nach bhfuil cead ag bodach súil a leagan ar iní an fhir fhiún-taigh"* (. . . "that a common lout has no right to look at a respectable man's daughter") becomes ". . . that a boorish land-slave has no such right. The worthless land-slave has no right in the world to look at the daughter of an honourable free-man!." . . .

It is not suggested that O'Flaherty is a bad translator, but that he deliberately tailored the English versions to suit his very wide and well-established reading public.

Note

1. A common asseveration in everyday speech.

Maureen O'Rourke Murphy

In his illuminating study of the stories of Liam O'Flaherty that have appeared in both English and Irish, Tomás de Bhaldraithe suggests that differences between versions are less a matter of translation than conscious changes for a wider English-speaking readership. . . . An examination of ten additional stories that have appeared both in Irish and English reveals a pattern in the differences that occur between versions of the same story. These differences suggest a certain self-consciousness about O'Flaherty's art in English which results in his ambivalent or defensive attitude toward his subjects and toward his audience.

The first group of stories deals with country people and most often focuses on a moment of passage: between childhood and adolescence, between adolescence and maturity, between life and death. Animal stories comprise the second group. Thematic differences are matters of emphasis but there are differences in characterization and style. The

From "The Double Vision of Liam O'Flaherty," *Éire-Ireland: A Journal of Irish Studies* 8, no. 3 (Fall 1973): 20–25. Reprinted by permission of the editor of *Éire-Ireland*, the Irish American Cultural Institute in St. Paul, Minnesota, and Professor Murphy.

tender moment of physical awareness in "An Scáthán" is made more explicitly sexual in "The Mirror." . . .

English versions stress the poverty of the island people more than their Irish counterparts. O'Flaherty's "great chain of hunger" image is common to both "Daoine Bochta" and to "Poor People" but compare Derrane simple tied to that chain in the Irish story with the prolixity of the English version: "without power, stricken, helpless, tied by the great chain of hunger." Intrusive comments like "poverty respects nothing" have no Irish equivalent. . . .

These additions are more noticeable still in "The Post Office," O'Flaherty's funniest story, one about three young people who try to send a Spanish telegram from a country post office in Connemara. The Irish version, like a yarn from *Peadar Chois Fharraige*, concentrates on the incompetence of the postmaster; the country people in the shop, like stock characters in an Abbey kitchen comedy, stare wide-eyed at the goings on. O'Flaherty's ambivalence toward the country people asserts itself in the English version of the story.

Religious piety is emphasized in English versions. When Derrane sees a full sea of seaweed he utters a low cry and runs toward the beach; in English he shouts "Praise be to God!" The father entering the bedroom to see his new son "Crossed himself and bent a knee to the new life and mother" in "Life." Little Jimmy wants to know the name of the saint who taught men how to make clothes, but in "The New Suit" it is so that he can pray to him that Needy stay sober until his suit is finished. . . .

On the other hand, while there is more religious piety in English versions, the Irish are often racier than their English counterparts. The midwife tells the mother in "An Beo," "Féachaigí uirthi féin agus i chomh onórach le maighdean" (Look at herself and she as proud as a new mother); in "Life" it becomes "Look at herself and she as frightened as a young girl on her wedding night." Máirtín's speech in "The Post Office" is rougher than in "Oifig an Phoist" or indeed rougher than one would hear in Connemara. . . . O'Flaherty maintains a lighter touch in "Oifig an Phoist." . . .

O'Flaherty's animal stories are more highly praised than his other stories for their simplicity and their clarity of vision, but here, too, the leaner Irish versions are often superior to their English counterparts in these qualities. In "The Cow's Death," the story O'Flaherty called "the best thing I have done," the cow is stupid. . . . "She stood stupidly looking at it a long time, without moving a muscle." There is no judgment in the later "Bás na Bó." The cow reacts to her missing calf with a mother's instinct, moving clumsily and with wonder and confusion but never stupidly. The outcome of the battle and the dénouement are inevitable in "An Chearc Uisce"; the large cock gives the champion's cry and the story ends as he approaches the hen. Suspenseful cries withhold the winner in "The Water Hen," but the large cock finally appears and the story ends with their coupling. In its English version the story is less a part of the cycle of nature than a seduction where clucks are triumphant and amorous, the cock steps proudly and elegantly and the hen is a coquette.

Besides additions O'Flaherty occasionally discards a natural image for something more pretentious in the English version. The kitten in "The Mouse" shakes his paws "díreach mar bheadh an talamh fliuch" (just as if the ground were wet) but in the later English version the kitten shakes his paw "to loosen the stricture of his muscle." . . .

Some of the additions to the English stories are very effective. The tension is heightened in "The New Suit" by Jimmy's worried prayers for a sober tailor, and that staple of the Irish countryside, the bargaining over a beast, is lengthened to add drama to "The Blow." In the latter, some of the effect is lost by O'Flaherty's pretentious diction. To call a halt to Éamonn's complaint about the price of pigs, Peadar shouts "If you mean business buy the pigs; if not run along home before I lose my temper with you. I never heard such scandalous talk in my life." A direct translation of the Irish of "An Buille," "If you are serious, buy the pigs. Otherwise go home without further talk" is closer to speech of the Irish countryman.

O'Flaherty is praised for his detachment and austerity; yet these qualities are superior in their Irish versions. The Irish stories are not without fault but [this] study reveals that the excesses, the offensive intrusions, the tedious repetitions, the faulty diction, and the structural slack are present in the English versions and missing in the Irish. Like many Irish writers, O'Flaherty filters his world to his English reader through the prism of his prose, but it is an Irish sensibility as a borrowed language. Often, when he is excessive, he directs his rage not at his Irish reader but on his behalf against the world.

William Daniels

When the present state of the general criticism of *Dúil* was examined, I found both Ó Buachalla and Máirtín Ó Cadhain calling it "perhaps the most remarkable collection of short stories in Irish."[1] It was unfortunate that they had not been asked to review the work almost twenty years earlier when it came out in 1953, rather than those hostile, shoot-from-the-hip writers like John Crawford who found O'Flaherty's Irish stories too simple, too "black and white,"[2] in their presentation of truth. . . . Reviews like Crawford's must have hurt the author, for Ó hEithir tells us that the publication of *Dúil* gave O'Flaherty more pleasure than that of any of his other books.[3]

Among critics who have written about O'Flaherty's Irish stories, de Bhaldraithe . . . objectively demonstrates O'Flaherty's fine adaptation of language to audience. But critics like Murphy too spiritedly adapt Frank O'Connor's belief that O'Flaherty's English "lacks the distinction and beauty of his Gaelic."[4] . . . Like Ó Cadhain, O'Faoláin has high praise for *Dúil*. "I know of very few instances in Irish writing, in either language, that welds the tender and the tough as consistently as O'Flaherty does."[5]

Critics writing in Irish like Breatnach, Ó Bauchalla, and Ó Dubhthaigh tend to call tough "energy" and tender "poetry."[6] . . . O'Flaherty himself was humble about this gift; he claimed that Ó Cadhain was the first writer in Irish to have described nature as it is, "the torments and the beauty that are together in life."[7] Every sensitive reader of *Dúil* must surely also notice that part of the joy in reading the stories comes from finding the tough and tender juxtaposed not only in one story but, through O'Flaherty's word repetitions, finding both tough and tender associated with each other across the stories. The 'rattle in the throat' (*"glothar ina scornach"*) of the excited child in "Dúil," for example, is heard also in the throat of the dying old man

From "Introduction to the Present State of Criticism of Liam O'Flaherty's Collection of Short Stories: *Dúil*," *Éire-Ireland: A Journal of Irish Studies* 23, no. 2 (Summer 1988): 124–32; reprinted by permission of the editor of *Éire-Ireland*, the Irish American Cultural Institute in St. Paul, Minnesota, and Professor Daniels.

of "An Beo." . . . Breatnach and, also, Mercier find *Dúil* demonstrates O'Flaherty's growing powers as he grew older, that his later stories were breaking new ground, and that he "might have begun a new and greater career in fiction after 1950."[8] John Kelleher agrees with Kilroy and Kelly that unfortunately O'Flaherty was "writing his best stories just when he stopped writing."[9] Kelly believes this is so because she finds situations nearly always dominating character in his early work while in his later stories what "counts is how a man conducts himself."[10] Because his later work is "less vehement and provocative," claims Kilroy, "some critics regard them as inferior to his earlier stories, but they treat subjects and attitudes that are more complex and subtle than such favored themes as brute struggle and resentment."[11]

None of the stories in *Dúil*, however, has received anything even approaching the sort of explication deserved by a writer of O'Flaherty's stature. . . . O'Flaherty was certainly not aware that his Irish readers would usually be given this book so early on in school that they would later assume it a young person's book; even the two books in Irish about *Dúil* clearly address an audience of critical first-readers. . . . Although Irish critics have worked with the volume as a whole, only Pádraic Breatnach recognizes that the "thinnest" stories in the volume gain in resonance when read as part of the volume as a whole.[12] But critics of the stories in both languages have been attracted by their sudden beginnings and swift endings. Kennelly admires their "crisp, definite" endings, yet Ó Dubhthaigh alone calls attention to the symbolic beginning of "Daoine Bochta."[13] O'Brien probably comes closest to suggesting the sort of explication that O'Flaherty's stories deserve when he says that "the effect of the narrative" in his shorter pieces "is similar to that of a lyric poem."[14]

From its title, of course, one expects *dúil* to be the volume's main theme; and O'Flaherty's use of the word centers around such definite words as *dúil, fonn* ('feeling'), and *tnúthán* ('longing'). Ó Cuagáin, the most disciplined and sensitive of O'Flaherty's critics writing in Irish, finds *Dúil* (desire) running through both human and animal characters in the stories, whether that of a girl for motherhood or of a dog to kill a rabbit.[15] Ó Dubhthaigh wisely suggests that we not forget to look for "desire without fulfillment." . . .

Among the early *Dúil* stories, mental frustration is found in both parents of "Daoine Bochta," for they can find nothing physical to fight against, while in the 1946 "Teangabháil," part of the tragedy for the young couple is that the boy cannot marry the girl without completely abandoning his dependent mother. The frustration of the two main characters in "Díoltas" is only relieved by death and/or revenge, while "Mearbhall" is possibly *Dúil's* most powerful recreation of frustration. . . .

While most of O'Flaherty's early critics recognized his penchant for violence, all found him lacking in humor. With the publication of *Dúil*, however, this immediately changed; unfortunately, however, the humor in such stories as "Oifig an Phoist" was often seen as an end in itself. . . . The early "An tAonach" exhibits a bitter irony as we share the people's joy in selling their cattle until we are reminded that they will end up in English bellies.

None of O'Flaherty's critics explores the settings of his stories in anything like detail. . . . We find island-like settings: the sea cliffs in "Bás na Bó," the field near the cliffs where sheep are shorn in "An Chulaith Nua," the rabbit's hole at the cliff edge in "An Fiach," lakes near the cliffs in "An Chearc Uisce" and "Uisce faoi Dhraíocht," a terrain of ledges like those on the Aran Islands in "Díoltas," strands where peasants gather seaweed in "Daoine Bochta" and "Teangabháil," and a home from which the family goes out to gather carrageen in "An Beo." Of the four other stories, "Oifig an Phoist" is on the coast road west of Galway, while the other three, "An Buille," "An tAonach," and "Mearbhall" seem set in or near Cois Fharraige towns.

As we would expect from the settings, most of the characters in *Dúil* are peasants. The only exceptions among the major characters are the little boy (and we could make a case for him) of the title story, the hotel-owner not far removed from the peasantry in "An Buille," the shop-tavern keeper in the little village of "Mearbhall," and, of course, the three tourists, one mysteriously native in speech and accent, who come to "Oifig an Phoist." Higgins writes of Synge and the gombeen men on the big island: "His hasty withdrawal . . . from Inishmore to Inishmaan [Inis Meáin] and his continuing to visit the middle island rather than the north are dictated by their presence. O'Flaherty, on the other hand, brought the new men into the foreground of his portrayal of island life." Yet in the above four stories, only Neidín's father in "An Buille" and the fanatical shop-tavern owner could even remotely be considered gombeen men.

Eleven of the remaining eighteen stories in *Dúil* touch on or feature peasants exclusively, while the main characters of the other three

stories are animals and a rock. . . . The typical islanders' attitude towards their animals is rather one of sympathy, like Neidín's for the
pigs, big and little, in "An Buille," the pedlar's love for his ass ("Díoltas"), the child's delight in the chickens ("An Beo"), the couple's for
their cow in "Bás na Bó," Cáit's for her mare in "Teangabháil," and
the narrator's and his wife's for the wild drake in "Uisce faoi
Dhraíocht." Trying not to confuse my own criticism with "applied nostalgia," I think of O'Flaherty's English "Parting" when I remember a
grandmother on the middle island unable to bring herself to see her
family's fourteen-year-old cow off at the quay after selling her. And
island dogs are not abused by their owners unless when pulling them
from the trouser legs of careless strangers. . . .

Critics of the Irish stories rarely address themselves to O'Flaherty's
handling of point of view; when they do, they usually echo the critics
of his English stories who blame him for his authorial intrusions. Even
so, neither group investigates the stories themselves closely enough for
their generalizations to do more than lure students into their own ex-
plorations. . . . I have found that a close explication of his Irish stories
usually reveals that, just because the narrative voice is in the first person, it should not be identified as O'Flaherty's.

O'Flaherty's skill in description, of course, has merited universal
praise. . . . But aren't his critics inconsistent in wishing to keep
O'Flaherty from "intruding" in his story while allowing him to change
camera angles, lenses, and filters at will?

Surveying O'Flaherty's early (1925), middle (1946), and late (1953)
Dúil stories, I have found that, although he uses dialogue in none of
his early stories, he does employ it in half of his middle group and in
four of his ten late stories. Because he uses dialogue earlier than some
critics think, not only should his "late" use of dialogue be studied more
carefully but his use of the spoken word in stories not so obviously built
upon dialogue demands critical scrutiny. . . .

In concluding this introduction to the present state of the general
criticism of Liam O'Flaherty's *Dúil* I have found that, although only
the critics of stories in Irish are qualified to discuss the author's figur-
ative use of that language, they have usually only echoed critics of his
English stories. . . . O'Flaherty's handling of symbolism in individual
stories has only been slightly touched on in "Dúil," "An Seabhac," "An
Scáthán," "Mearbhall," and "An Buille."

O'Flaherty's *Dúil* deserves much better than it has received from critics in both Irish and English; each story needs to be explicated and related to the other stories in the volume. And I would suggest that scholars of modern Irish literature who do not know modern Irish itself should not wait around until their fifties as I did, but should begin that study now. After sifting and resifting the scholarship on Yeats and Joyce, to read *Dúil* and to realize how much work needs to be done with it should rekindle that joy we once found as young graduate students on coming into a relatively unexplored field. Especially when we recognize that in learning Irish we create a solid foundation on which to rebuild our understanding even of those writers from Ireland who have used English, in whole or in part, as their medium.

Notes

1. Breandán Ó Buachalla, "Ó Cadhain, Ó Céileachair, Ó Flaithearta," *Comhar* 25 (Bealtaine [May] 1967): 75; Máirtín Ó Cadhain, "Irish Prose in the Twentieth Century," in *Literature in Celtic Countries*, ed. J. E. Caerwyn Williams (Cardiff: University of Wales Press, 1971), 146.

2. John Crawford, "Liam O'Flaherty's Black and White World," *Irish Press*, 1 August 1953, 4.

3. Breandán Ó hEithir, "Liam Ó Flatharta agus a Dhúchas" [Liam O'Flaherty and his heritage], in *Willie the Plain Pint—agus an Pápa* [Willie the plain pint—and the pope] (Dublin and Cork: Cló Mercier, 1977), 76.

4. Frank O'Connor, "A Good Short Story Must Be News," *New York Times Book Review*, 10 June 1956, 20.

5. Seán Ó Faoláin, *"Dúil,"* in *The Pleasures of Gaelic Literature*, ed. John Jordan (Dublin: Mercier, 1977), 116–17.

6. Pádraic Breatnach, *Nótaí ar* Dúil (Notes on *Dúil*) (Cork: Cló Mercier, 1971); Ó Buachalla, "Ó Cadhain, Ó Céileachair, Ó Flaithearta"; Fiachra Ó Dubhthaigh, *Leargas ar* Dúil *Uí Fhlaithearta* (Insight into O'Flaherty's *Dúil*) (Dublin: Foilseacháin Náisiúnta, 1981).

7. *"An Braon Broghach"* (The dirty drop), *Comhar* 8 (Bealtaine [May] 1949): 30.

8. Vivian Mercier, "Man Against Nature: The Novels of Liam O'Flaherty," *Wascana Review* 1, no. 2 (1966): 45.

9. John Kelleher, interview, Chatham, Massachusetts, June 1986.

10. Angeline A. Kelly, *Liam O'Flaherty the Storyteller* (London: Macmillan, 1976), 113.

11. James F. Kilroy, "Setting the Standards: Writers of the 1920s and 1930s," in *The Irish Short Story: A Critical History*, ed. Kilroy (Boston: Twayne, 1984), 103.

12. Breatnach, 29.

Chronology

1896	Liam O'Flaherty born 28 August in Gort na gCapall near Kilmurvey in the middle of Inis Mór, the largest of the three Aran Islands.
1908–1913	Studies at Rockwell College, Cashel, County Tipperary.
1913–1914	Studies at Blackrock College, County Dublin.
1914	Studies at Holy Cross diocesan seminary in Dublin from September to November.
1914–1915	Studies at University College, Dublin.
1915–1917	Enlists (under the name of Bill Ganly) in the Irish Guards of the British army and fights in Belgium and France, where he is wounded in September 1917.
1918–1920	"Two Years" of wandering and work in London, South America, Canada, and the United States.
1921–1922	Return to Aran followed by Republican activism in Dublin, culminating in the occupation of the Rotunda in January 1922.
1923	Publication of earliest stories and first novel, *Thy Neighbour's Wife*.
1923–1932	Correspondence and friendship with Edward Garnett.
1924	First volume of stories, *Spring Sowing*.
1925	*The Informer*.
1926	Marries Margaret Barrington.
1929	*The Mountain Tavern and Other Stories* and *A Tourist's Guide to Ireland*.
1930	*Two Years*.
1931	*The Ecstasy of Angus* and *I Went to Russia*.
1932	Separation from Margaret Barrington. *Skerrett*.
1934	*Shame the Devil*.
1937	*The Short Stories of Liam O'Flaherty* and *Famine*.

1940–1946   Lives in Connecticut, South America, and the Caribbean, returning to Dublin more or less for good in 1946.

1948   *Two Lovely Beasts and Other Stories*.

1953   *Dúil*, O'Flaherty's sole volume of stories in Irish.

1956   *The Stories of Liam O'Flaherty*.

1976   *The Pedlar's Revenge and Other Stories*.

1984   O'Flaherty dies 7 September.

Bibliography

This bibliography is intended as a concise reader's guide to the most important sources for an understanding of O'Flaherty's short fiction. I suggest that the reader also consult the bibliography at the end of Angeline Kelly's book (listed below), which details the periodical and anthology appearances of most of O'Flaherty's stories and clarifies the contents of each of his collections of stories in English. I have made no attempt to be as comprehensive as she is in listing bibliographical items in English, but I do include important sources not listed by Kelly, such as criticism published since 1976 and more criticism in Irish. A number of additional sources are cited in the notes to part 1.

Primary Works

Short Fiction

Dúil. Dublin: Sáirséal agus Dill, 1953.
The Ecstasy of Angus. 1931. Reprint. Dublin: Wolfhound, 1978.
The Mountain Tavern and Other Stories. New York: Harcourt, 1929.
Short Stories. Dublin: Wolfhound, 1986. Originally published by Wolfhound Press in 1976 as *The Pedlar's Revenge and Other Stories*.
The Short Stories of Liam O'Flaherty. 1937. Reprint. Kent, England: New English Library, 1986.
Spring Sowing. London: Cape, 1924.
The Stories of Liam O'Flaherty. New York: Devin-Adair, 1956.
The Tent. London: Cape, 1926.
Two Lovely Beasts. 1948. Reprint. New York: Devin-Adair, 1950.
The Wounded Cormorant and Other Stories. New York: Norton, 1973.

Nonfiction

A Cure for Unemployment. London: E. Lahr, 1931.
I Went to Russia. New York: Harcourt, 1931.
Joseph Conrad: An Appreciation. London: Lahr, 1930.
The Life of Tim Healy. London: Jonathan Cape, 1927.

Bibliography

Shame the Devil. 1934. Reprint. Dublin: Wolfhound Press, 1981.
A Tourist's Guide to Ireland. London: Mandrake, 1929.
Two Years. London: Cape, 1930.

Unpublished Manuscript Sources

The Liam O'Flaherty Collection. Harry Ransom Humanities Research Center at the University of Texas at Austin.

Secondary Works

Averill, Deborah M. "Liam O'Flaherty." In *The Irish Short Story from George Moore to Frank O'Connor,* 111–52. Washington: University Press of America, 1982.
Breatnach, Pádraic. *Nótaí ar* Dúil (Notes on *Dúil*). Cork: Cló Mercier, 1971.
Daniels, William. "The Diction of Desire: Liam O'Flaherty's 'Dúil'." *Éire-Ireland: A Journal of Irish Studies* 24, no. 4 (Winter 1989): 75–88.
———. "Introduction to the Present State of Criticism of Liam O'Flaherty's Collection of Short Stories: *Dúil.*" *Éire-Ireland* 23, no. 2 (Summer 1988): 124–32.
De Bhaldraithe, Tomás. "Liam O'Flaherty—Translator (?)." *Éire-Ireland* 3, no. 2 (Summer 1968): 149–53.
———. "Ó Flaitheartaigh agus Léirmheastóirí Eile" (O'Flaherty and other critics). *Irish Times,* 22 November 1984, 10.
Doyle, Paul A. *Liam O'Flaherty.* New York: Twayne Publishers, 1971.
Eckley, Grace. "Liam O'Flaherty." *Critical Survey of Short Fiction* 5 (1981): 2005–11.
Kelly, Angeline A. *Liam O'Flaherty the Storyteller.* London: Macmillan, 1976.
Kennelly, Brendan. "Liam O'Flaherty: The Unchained Storm, a View of His Short Stories." In *The Irish Short Story,* edited by Patrick Rafroidi and Terence Brown, 175–87. Gerrards Cross, England: Colin Smythe; Atlantic Highlands, N.J.: Humanities Press, 1979.
Kiely, Benedict. "Liam O'Flaherty: A Story of Discontent." *Month* (Dublin) 2, no. 5 (September 1949): 184–93.
Mercier, Vivian. "The Irish Short Story and Oral Tradition." In *The Celtic Cross: Studies in Irish Culture and Literature,* edited by Ray B. Browne, William John Rosselli, and John Loftus, 98–116. West Lafayette, Ind.: Purdue University Press, 1964.
———. "Man against Nature: The Novels of Liam O'Flaherty." *Wascana Review* 1, no. 2 (1966): 37–46.
Murphy, Maureen O'Rourke. "The Double Vision of Liam O'Flaherty." *Éire-Ireland* 8, no. 3 (Fall 1973): 20–25.

————. "'The Salted Goat': Devil's Bargain or Fable of Faithfulness." *Canadian Journal of Irish Studies* 5, no. 2 (1979): 60–61.

————. "The Short Story in Irish." *Mosaic: a Journal for the Comparative Study of Literature and Ideas* 12, no. 3 (1979): 81–89.

Murray, Michael H. "Liam O'Flaherty and the Speaking Voice." *Studies in Short Fiction* 5, no. 2 (1968): 154–62.

O'Brien, James H. *Liam O'Flaherty.* Lewisburg, Pa.: Bucknell University Press, 1973.

Ó Buachalla, Breandán. "Ó Cadhain, Ó Céileachair, Ó Flaithearta." *Comhar* 25 (May 1967): 69–73.

O'Connor, Frank. "A Good Short Story Must Be News." Review of *The Short Stories of Liam O'Flaherty. New York Times Book Review*, 10 June 1956, 1, 20.

O'Connor, Helene. "Liam O'Flaherty: Literary Ecologist." *Éire-Ireland* 7, no. 2 (Summer 1972): 47–54.

Ó Cuagáin, Proinsias. "Dúil san Ainmhí: Téama i Scéalta Liam Ó Flaithearta" (Desire in the animal: A theme in Liam O'Flaherty's stories). *Irisleabhar Mhá Nuad* (Maynooth Journal) (1968): 49–55, 57–59.

Ó Dubhthaigh, Fiachra. *Léargas ar Dúil Uí Fhlaithearta* (Insight into O'Flaherty's *Dúil*). Dublin: Foilseacháin Náisiúnta, 1981.

Ó Faoláin, Seán. "Don Quixote O'Flaherty." *London Mercury* 37 (December 1937): 170–75. Revised edition, *Bell* 2 (June 1941): 28–36.

Ó hEithir, Breandán. "Liam Ó Flatharta agus a Dhúchas" (Liam O'Flaherty and his heritage). In *Willie the Plain Pint—Agus an Pápa* (Willie the Plain Pint—and the pope), 65–76. Dublin: Cló Mercier, 1977.

Saul, George Brandon. "A Wild Sowing: The Short Stories of Liam O'Flaherty." *Review of English Literature* 4 (July 1963): 108–13.

Sheeran, Patrick F. *The Novels of Liam O'Flaherty: A Study in Romantic Realism.* Atlantic Highlands, N.J.: Humanities Press, 1976.

Thompson, Richard J. "The Sage Who Deep in Central Nature Delves: Liam O'Flaherty's Short Stories." *Éire-Ireland* 18, no. 1 (Spring 1983): 80–97.

Washburn, Judith. "Objective Narration in Liam O'Flaherty's Short Stories." *Éire-Ireland* 24, no. 3 (Fall 1989): 120–25.

Zneimer, John. *The Literary Vision of Liam O'Flaherty.* Syracuse, N.Y.: Syracuse University Press, 1970.

Index

The Author

James M. Cahalan teaches in the English Department at Indiana University of Pennsylvania where he has directed the doctoral program in literature and criticism. He previously directed both the Irish Studies Program at the University of Massachusetts–Boston and the Dublin Program of IUP's Center for International Studies. He earned his B.A. at New College in Sarasota, Florida; his M.A. (on a Fulbright fellowship) at University College, Dublin, with first-class honors; and his Ph.D. at the University of Cincinnati. He is the author of *Great Hatred, Little Room: The Irish Historical Novel* (1983), *The Irish Novel: A Critical History* (1988), and numerous articles and reviews about Irish literature, folklore, and history.

The Editor

Gordon Weaver earned his Ph.D. in English and creative writing at the University of Denver, and is currently professor of English at Oklahoma State University. He is the author of several novels, including *Count a Lonely Cadence, Give Him a Stone, Circling Byzantium,* and most recently *The Eight Corners of the World.* His short stories are collected in *The Entombed Man of Thule, Such Waltzing Was Not Easy, Getting Serious, Morality Play,* and *A World Quite Round.* Recognition of his fiction includes the St. Lawrence Award for Fiction (1973), two National Endowment for the Arts fellowships (1974 and 1989), and the O. Henry First Prize (1979). He edited *The American Short Story, 1945–1980: A Critical History* and is currently editor of the *Cimarron Review.* Married and the father of three daughters, he lives in Stillwater, Oklahoma.